IMPROVE YOUR SOCIAL SKILLS

Learn How to Stop Procrastination through Improving Your Conversations and Fostering Genuine Relationships

© Written By Daniel Anderson

Table of Contents

Introduction To Social Skills 3

Social Skills - Living and Surviving in the Society .. 14

Manage Shyness 27

Improve Your Conversations 44

Build Genuine Relationships 60

Body Language 72

Stop Procrastinating 89

How To Dominate People 103

Building Confidence 110

Make Friends without Giving Up Who You Are 123

Conclusion 133

Introduction To Social Skills

What you are about to discover in this EBook is the most comprehensive and eye-opening content written about improving social skills. This is the ultimate guide that equips you from A to Z about everything you need to understand about social skills and how it can be improved. Regardless of whether you are an introvert who finds it hard to socialize or an extrovert who looks to improve his/her social skills, there are lots of surprising insights for you to learn here. I hope you enjoy reading this EBook and while doing so, uncover the secrets to improving your social skills and taking your life to the next level. First of all, before I take you through ways in which you can improve your social skills, let's look at the meaning of social skills and its basics.

What are Social Skills?

Social skills are described as definite approaches applied by an individual to carry out social functions effectively and eventually be regarded as socially acceptable. Your behavior and interactions with others are indicators that reveal your status in the community you are in, if you are likely to be a friend or partner, and more importantly if they see you as a future potential asset to a company.

Good social skills are an essential part of building rich

friendships, enjoying yourself in public, and succeeding in your career. If you consider yourself an introvert, it can be hard to engage in conversation with people you don't know. Luckily, the more you practice being social, the easier it will become.

In practical terms, what are social skills?

- A one on one communication where listening is a give and take interaction and each party intends to understand the messages conveyed.

- A skill that is acquired through continuous learning. As you interact, you begin to learn the aspects of the personality of the person you are talking to. You start to understand the person as to where he or she is coming from, and you try to put yourself in his shoes as he relates to his past experiences. You can draw out impressions of what he is like, and you try to act in a way that is within the appropriate norms.

- Socials skills have two aspects - verbal and non-verbal. A person with excellent verbal, social skills knows how to say the appropriate things at the right time, can communicate freely and get the conversation flowing smoothly, He/She is capable of using the proper vocal tone and quality and able to convey the message intelligently and understandably.

While a person with good non-verbal skills knows how to use bodily movement at an appropriate time, your gestures enable you to convey your message clearly through actions. Your posture, your eye contact, your voice tone, and facial expression are non-verbal social skills. Please take note that too many gestures can overkill. Do not overdo it.

- Social skills are influenced by culture and by a particular social group. A person's social skills are based on how he or she was brought up. Most often, our behavior is brought about by our culture. A person's social skills differ from one another. A kiss and hug on the cheek as a welcome gesture may not be a socially accepted gesture in some conservative countries.

How you behave during interactions, how you put your words together, your adaptability to the environment you are in, and the way you handle matters at hand are factors that determine how your personality is judged. It is not enough to have a ready smile and feel confident. It's not about looks; it's not about what you know that draws people to like you. It is all about who you are, what you do, how you do things and how others see you that you are judged. Learning what social skills are will help you get the reward of feeling accepted. Step forward and be recognized.

Social Skill Basics

Navigating the social world requires a certain degree of social awareness. Improving social skills does not end when you are an adult. You are always learning and adapting, even on a subliminal level, no matter what your age.

Children, on the other hand, do not have the experiences

that adults have had and quite often do not understand why they have to see, do and say certain things that they don't want to.

Even as adults, with all our worldliness and maturity, do not fully appreciate how social etiquettes have changed over the last few years. For example, there are certain times and places to use your phone, or how to converse in the multimedia world.

However, three things are certain when developing and maintaining your social skills.

1. Seeing

Seeing entails finding your social cues. Notice the context of your situation. Is it casual or formal? Are the people around you acquaintances, strangers of casual friends? Different situations call for different kinds of behavior. Good judgment is necessary when you are social seeing. Notice how people around you conduct themselves and monitor their reactions to various situations. Basically, by social seeing, you are subliminally avoiding inappropriate actions or reactions.

2. Thinking

The second of these social skill basics involves interpreting other people's behavior and understanding why they are doing what they are doing. It also consists of predicting possible responses and coming up with effective ways of dealing with a situation or person.

If you struggle socially, it is quite indicative when you misinterpret other's intentions and are not able to immediately come up with constructive ways to resolve any social difficulty.

3. Doing

This is about interacting with people positively. Quite often we know what we should do, but experience difficulty in actually doing it. We might want to join a discussion group, for example, but freeze up and feel anxious in the social context of the situation. We either find ourselves being very self-conscious or totally embarrassed. If you are not socially aware, you might also speak impulsively. It is essential to hold a conversation at least or join into one.

These three social skill basics are essential in creating and maintaining all the different social skills.

Being enthusiastic and loud might not be the best way to handle a situation that requires quiet decorum. Social skills are about having the ability to adjust your behavior and be flexible in any situation.

Social skills are defined in various ways but are a necessary ability to get along with people and maintain fulfilling relationships.

Are you a socially awkward person?

Should you embrace your social awkwardness in social settings? Is it just a part of who you are? Some people will tell you to embrace it, but I genuinely feel that it's important to try and overcome being socially awkward as much as possible, especially if you want to create a life full of relationships, love, happiness, and success.

Being socially awkward will affect your life negatively. It may not affect your online presence, where you can say whatever is on your mind without fear of hearing a reply and where you can delete any word or statement you make. But, it will affect your ability to form real relationships with family, friends, and co-workers, and it will affect your self-esteem, success, and happiness in the long run.

The bottom line is that when you are socially awkward, you feel awkward or out of place, and that makes all situations and events with other people more difficult than they need to be. Moreover, it can hold you back from going after things you want because, often, the things you want are through or around other people, which can be hard to face.

Therefore, I highly suggest that you embrace your social awkwardness as a part of who you are now and then find a way to improve your social skills so you can become less socially awkward. All the information you need to improve your social skills is in this book.

10 Signs That You Are Socially Awkward

Are you not sure if you are socially awkward? Following are some shared experiences awkward people have. If you find that you relate to almost all of them, then you are socially awkward and need to work on it if you want to change your relationships and life around.

1. People Avoid You In Social Settings

If you find people moving away from you or avoiding you during social settings, then there is a high chance that you are socially awkward. People don't feel comfortable around people who are awkward and lack social skills. It's hard to have a conversation with them, understand what they are trying to convey, and feel at ease around them. This is true whether you are at work or in another social setting.

2. You Avoid People As Often As Possible

If you ever find yourself ducking behind something to hide from someone that you would have to chat with, or crossing the street to avoid someone, or quickly shutting the elevator so that you don't have to talk to your co-worker, or canceling plans where you will need to interact with people, then you are probably socially awkward. We avoid people because we feel uncomfortable at the thought of having to engage with them.

3. Dates Always Go Bad

If you find yourself offending or scaring off almost every date you have, then there is a high chance that you are doing things that are weird or looked down upon by someone who is looking for love. A lot of socially awkward people don't understand what other people are looking for or find unacceptable.

For instance, you could be talking over your date, ignoring their questions, saying offensive things, asking inappropriate questions, or acting in a manner that makes them think you are too needy or desperate. Without being there with you, it's hard to tell exactly what you are doing wrong, but it's easy to say that something is going wrong if all your dates never lead into anything else.

4. Romantic Relationships Don't Last Long

You may find someone who can look past your awkwardness, but after a while, they start to grow tired of your inappropriate behavior or inability to be social and have a good time. They will probably tell you straight up during your relationship that they wish you were more social and outgoing. And, eventually, when things don't change, they leave.

5. You Don't Have A Lot Of Friends

Friendships are hard for you. You don't make friends easily, and when you do, you often lose them because you are not willing to meet their friends or go out and do things with them. You would rather sit at home with them than go out, which is a friendship-killer because friends build experiences in life and bond over those experiences.

6. Your Self-Esteem Is Affected By How Others Treat You

If your self-esteem goes up and down faster than a rollercoaster while you are in a social setting, even if you are not talking to anyone, then you are probably socially awkward. It means you are sizing up how other people feel about you through what they say and do, and then letting your conclusions – whether they are based in reality or not – dictate how you feel about yourself.

7. You Overthink All Social Instances

Big or small, you replay the moments in your day where you needed to relate to other people, and you beat yourself up over them. For instance, if you talked for a few seconds to someone about nothing important, you may not be able to stop thinking about whether or not you were friendly enough or stop worrying about what they thought about you.

8. You Are Scared Of Being Seen In A Negative Way

Are you scared that other people are going to see you negatively? Maybe they will think you are not funny, annoying, ugly, too sad, too happy, too fat, too thin, not smart enough, or not witty enough. If you think about these things before you even get into a social situation and have said a word, then that is a big sign that you are socially awkward. The very thought of being a social makes you uncomfortable because you care too much about how people view you.

9. People Tell You That You Are Weird

If people are outright telling you that you are weird, rude, annoying, or frustrating, then there is a good chance that you don't understand social norms and are rubbing people the wrong way. While these people can easily make you feel bad about yourself, they are also being honest with you and giving you criticism that can help you become less awkward and more confident if you embrace what they are saying.

For instance, if someone tells you that you are annoying, then you have a chance to work on some personal growth. You may want to look at how you interact with others. Do you take the time to get to know other people? Do you act appropriately around other people? Do you say things that are off the wall and don't need to be said? If you can find answers, then you can begin to fix issues that you may be having in social settings that make you annoying and then form stronger and healthier relationships with people.

10. You Have A Different Impact Than You Meant To Have

You try to convey how much you like someone, and you

end up offending them. Or, you try to make someone feel better, and you end up making them feel worse. If you always find that you are not doing what you set out to do, then that is a huge sign that you are socially awkward.

OK. These are the ten signs of socially awkward individuals. Taking them into consideration, this is the right moment to ask yourself again "Am I socially awkward?"

Social Skills - Living and Surviving in the Society

Right from the time we are very young, we begin to learn the basics in social skills, which are, learning how to live with, communicate with, and get along with the people around you. If you have siblings, those basic skills come into play quite quickly; sharing of toys and sharing a room with a brother or sister. As we grow older and begin school, those skills become even more important as you must now share your space with many more people. Children who have not been adequately prepared for such an event may find it difficult to adjust to this new society they have become a part of.

To define the meaning of proper social skills, you would have to consider the environment or society you are living in. What works in one society doesn't necessarily work in another; none-the-less, basic social skills are imperative to live a happy and enjoyable life among others in your community, workplace, and home life. It is, in a nutshell, the manner at which we participate and conduct ourselves within society; what is right and what is wrong pertaining to the society in which you live.

In order to fit into society, society expects each person to act in a manner that doesn't go against social norms. Being rude to another person, cursing in public, disrespectful behavior is all negative aspects of not having proper social skills. The more significant part of most societies learn these skills early in life, and they are carried over into their adult life; however, there are some who tend to go against the grain of society and lack the social skills that most of us don't even have to think about; we just know how to act appropriately. There are also people who have a basic understanding of this concept but aren't sure how to become better at practicing their social skills in public situations.

For Example, when employers interview people, they aren't just looking at their credentials; they are evaluating how they interact with the employer. They look for signs and ask questions on certain topics requiring a social interaction to see if the one being interviewed has a good understanding of social skills as to how they would handle a delicate situation. The lack of such skills could mean the difference in getting the job or not getting the job; one must be able to conduct themselves respectfully and adequately in the workplace and among others in society.

Having good social skills gives you an advantage in society; people are attracted to those who display proper social behavior and don't feel uncomfortable in engaging in conversation with you. Having proper social skills is simply knowing how to be respectful, courteous, and understanding what society considers as the norm.

Helping children learn social skills

Some kids seem to learn social skills quickly, but others can benefit from some extra coaching. Almost every child struggles with friendship issues at some time in some way, whether it's trying to find a buddy in a new school, handling teasing, or having an argument with a friend. These kinds of experiences are very common, but they can also be very painful.

Considering the three processes underlying social skills — seeing, thinking, and doing — can help you understand where your child might be stuck and suggest ways to help your child move forward. For instance, during a play date or a trip to the playground, you might be able to help your child see more effectively by making observations that draw your child's attention to relevant cues (e.g., "Mike seems frustrated right now." "Scott and Abigail are taking turns on the slide.").

If your child is struggling to figure out how to respond to a social dilemma, you might be able to support your child's social thinking by providing insights to explain the other child's behavior. You could also help your child brainstorm possible responses and evaluate their likely outcomes.

Finally, you might be able to create opportunities for your child to practice "doing" social skills by role-playing tricky situations, planning strategies ahead of time for tough situations, or arranging appropriate activities.

For instance, children who find it hard to make eye contact may find it easier to "look at people between the eyebrows." This comes across the same as eye contact but may feel less threatening for children.

Rehearsing simple responses to common questions can also help anxious children get past deer-in-the-headlight moments. "How was your weekend?" "Good. I had a soccer game." "How's school?" "Good. We're learning about the Mayans in Social Studies." These exchanges are a good way to handle predictable questions.

Kids often make friends by doing things together, so an interest-related club, class, or team might be helpful. One-on-one play dates often feel more manageable than group activities for children who are on the shy side. Some children who struggle socially with their age-mates do better with children who are a few years younger or older than they are.

Continually experiencing social failure doesn't help children learn. Children who struggle with friendship issues need guidance and support so they can "get it right" socially by seeing, thinking, and doing in ways that help them connect with their peers. Getting lots of practice having positive interactions with other kids enables children to feel genuinely comfortable, competent, and confident in social situations.

How Good Social Skills Contribute To School Success

Well developed social skills are among the major factors which contribute to school success. Positive social and behavioral competence correlates with peer acceptance, teacher and parent approval, and academic success. Poor social skill and maladaptive behaviors in the classroom correlate with school failure, higher drop out rates, social rejection, and decreased self-esteem.

Social skills are very specific behaviors which allow us to behave appropriately in different environmental setting and which help us develop positive relationships with others. Most of us learn these skills automatically through observation and participation in family and school life. However, some children do not learn social skills through general, non-directive strategies and require targeted instruction in order to understand and use these techniques effectively. This is particularly true for students who have learning disabilities. signs of poor social skills development include, among others, classroom behaviors such as defiance, disturbing other children, and inadequate independent work habits. With peers, one might notice problems such as aggressive behaviors, bragging, shyness, bossiness, and temper tantrums.

It is important to listen carefully when school personnel suggests that your child has peer relation difficulties or problem behaviors in the classroom. Some public school systems have short term counseling programs which offer social skills training in small groups for students who are at risk. However, many do not, and parents should be aware that they serve as the child's first teacher in the area of social skills development. Research indicates that social skills can be improved if specifically taught and practiced in a variety of environmental settings. The mall, restaurant, baseball field, and Grandma's house can all serve as teaching opportunities for the concerned parent. Natural settings can provide powerful reinforcement of appropriate behaviors which increases the likelihood of those behaviors being used in the future.

Thorough observation will determine whether your child is lacking a specific skill or is unable to use a known skill effectively. If lacking the skill, such as starting a conversation or entering a group, parents can help through the use of specific instruction, practice, and feedback. If the child knows the skill or behavior and is not applying it, the parent can help by developing a behavior plan which provides opportunities for practice and reinforcement of the desired behaviors, while reducing the occurrence of undesirable or maladaptive behaviors. an example of the latter is using good social problem-solving skills instead of engaging in temper tantrums or aggression towards peers.

Learning good social skills is a lengthy developmental process. Changing existing patterns of social interactions is often a complicated task. But good social and behavioral skills are critical indicators of children's later social, occupational, and psychological adjustment. Parents can help by intervening early when problems begin to arise. Skills which are taught explicitly in a variety of natural settings are frequently learned faster and used more consistently across settings. By teaching social skills, parents are providing the child with life skills which will be beneficial in the classroom and the word of work beyond.

How Good Social Skills Contribute to Business Success

Strong social skills are the difference between a good business person and a great one. Yet in business, the importance of social skills are often overlooked and neglected.

Universities and business schools do not formally teach social skills in their curriculum. It is expected the "soft skills" you need to interact effectively with other team members will be learned on-the-job or through corporate training initiatives.

However, when companies and human resource departments choose corporate training for their employees, they often prefer to invest in developing their employee's technical skill rather than their interpersonal or social skills.

Technical skill is important. It allows you to complete the tasks required for your job. However technical skill alone will not make a great business person.

A great business person will always go one step further and strive for the rare combination of technical plus social skill. They understand that by improving their ability to interact with other team members and clients, they can get the job done faster, more efficiently and cost-effectively.

In essence, by having a strong level of social skill, a higher level than your peers, you can increase the amount of value you add to the company. For employees, this could mean more promotions. For entrepreneurs, this could mean more clients.

As an Author in this niche, I create books like this for professionals who want to improve their social skills. Specifically, they want to know how to project more confidence in business, how to start and continue a conversation, and how to show their professional competence and worth.

Mastering these skills is the difference between a good business person and a great one.

In this section, I want to share with you 22 reasons why as a professional or entrepreneur, you need a strong level of social skills in business.

1. Social skills help you give a good first impression because you know how to present yourself positively and form a connection with others.

2. Social skills help you start a conversation with somebody new in your office which can lead to better relations with your coworkers and a happier work environment.

3. Social skills help you start a conversation with a potential client which can lead to increased sales.

4. Social skills help you identify the right outfit to wear in the office and at business events so you establish the professional image you want to be known for.

5. Social skills help you walk into a networking event with poise and confidence because you know the right body language to use.

6. Social skills help you choose who to talk with at a networking event so you can form the right connections in business.

7. Social skills help you connect better with your coworkers, clients, and boss because you know how to hold conversations and interact positively with others.

8. Social skills help you to get others to know, like and trust you because you know the exact steps to build each element.

9. Social skills help you build a leadership reputation because you will look and feel more comfortable and confident in business situations.

10. Social skills help you build a strong professional brand because you know how to establish a consistently high level of presentation and interaction with others.

11. Social skills help you interact politely and professionally on social media and help you avoid damage to your professional reputation.

12. Social skills help you deal with conversation pitfalls such as an interrupter or a conversation hog.

13. Social skills help you remember and use names in conversation which will, in turn, help others to like you.

14. Social skills help you offer the right handshake for business and as a result, convey the right message to others.

15. Social skills help you exchange business cards with respect so you make that person feel important and appreciated.

16. Social skills help you understand the hierarchy of your company and the chain of command, which will help you navigate the corporate environment.

17. Social skills help you understand the dangers of extreme levels of know, like and trust so you can avoid damaging your professional reputation.

18. Social skills help you prepare for networking events so you can approach each networking event with strategy, focus, and fewer nerves.

19. Social skills help you work more efficiently and effectively in a team, leading to a more harmonious and happier work environment.

20. Social skills boost your team's productivity and therefore help your business become more profitable.

21. Social skills help entrepreneurs connect better with clients, leading to more contracts and increased profits.

22. Social skills will make you feel more comfortable in business situations (because you know what to do), and as a result, more confident.

As a high-achieving professional or entrepreneur, which reason resonates with you the most?

How the Seduction Community Is Screwing Up Your Social Skills

When most guys join the seduction community, they are on a mission to improve their dating skills with women. Unfortunately, there "side effects" to joining the community that most of the gurus don't tell you about in the fine print. While most guys join with the seduction community sincere desire to improve their social skills, the fact of the matter is there is a very strong correlation between joining the seduction community and adopting weird behaviors. I'm going to talk about some of the side effects of the seduction community in this section.

1. Female Validation Addiction

The first side effect of the seduction community is that you get addicted to getting validation from girls. This, of course, doesn't seem like a big deal when you're out sarging for months, but when you finally chill out and build a social circle, people get this weird vibe. Most people can't put words to it, but it's the vibe of, you constantly trying to manipulate women, even when you don't even like them when a normal guy would just be relaxed.

Guys become addicted to the validation of women. I had a friend who used to frown upon guys who drank and smoked weed in order to "feel good" until he realized that he got to a point where unless he made out with one or two women when he went out, he would consider that a bad night.

Doesn't anyone else see how unhealthy thinking like this is?

2. Pickup Skills Don't Equal Social Skills

Think of it like this, in tenth-grade geometry, I learned that a square is a rectangle, but a rectangle is not a square. In the real world, pick up skills equal social skills, but social skills do not equally pick up skills. Social skills are a much broader concept. Knowing how to seduce a woman, unfortunately, will not solve your life's problems.

A common symptom that I've seen and heard from other guys on campus, is that after joining the seduction community, they have a very hard time making friends with guys. Why is this occurring? Because the seduction community doesn't cover a chapter on how to be a chill guy (although several people teach how to steal a cool guy's girlfriend). This has been a big sticking point for guys, and I think it's evidence of weak overall social skills.

3. Skewed Beliefs About Women

The seduction community also pumps some unbelievably skewed beliefs about women. While it is true that women are sexual creatures. The seduction community has promoted the idea that women are into flings with guys that they just met and don't know. I think this is the exception, not the rule.

I think that outside of the cold approach scene, where 99% of everyone else gets laid when a woman is attracted to a guy, she almost universally considers the future implications of hooking up with this guy. More often than not, she would rather have a single commitment than a random fling.

Within a social circle setting, this dynamic becomes much more obvious. Sometimes the courtship spans out over long periods of time simply due to logistics. It's the PUA nerd who's read too many eBooks, who tries to force the close on day three because he thinks it MUST happen then. This is not strictly true in the social circle game. In cold approach, her attraction for you evaporates like a vapor. In social circle game, your attraction is static, because your value is static.

My biggest "ah ha" was that social skills are bigger and more important than picking up skills. A guy who is high status, and has many high-status friends who are both male and female, typically does not have too much trouble getting a date. He doesn't need to spend thousands of hours listening to programs and cold approaching night after night. He also does not have any of the weird side effects that come from being stuck in the seduction community mindset for too long. He is chill, he is fun, he is dominant, he is social.

Manage Shyness

Are you shy and self-conscious in social situations? Do you feel isolated and lonely, but unsure how to connect with others? You may feel like you're the only one, but the truth is that lots of people struggle with shyness and social insecurity. No matter how awkward or nervous you feel in the company of others, you can learn to silence self-critical thoughts, boost your self-esteem, and become more confident in your interactions with others. You don't have to change your personality, but by learning new skills and adopting a different outlook you can overcome your fears and build rewarding friendships.

Do you need help dealing with shyness and loneliness?

As humans, we're meant to be social creatures. Having friends makes us happier and healthier—in fact, being socially connected is key to our mental and emotional health. Yet many of us are shy and socially introverted. We feel awkward around unfamiliar people, unsure of what to say, or worried about what others might think of us. This can cause us to avoid social situations, cut ourselves off from others, and gradually become isolated and lonely.

Loneliness is a common problem among people of all ages and backgrounds, and yet it's something that most of us hesitate to admit. But loneliness is nothing to feel ashamed about. Sometimes, it's a result of external circumstances:

you've moved to a new area, for example. In such cases, there are lots of steps you can take to meet new people and turn acquaintances into friends.

But what if you're struggling with shyness, social insecurity, or a long-standing difficulty making friends? The truth is that none of us are born with social skills. They're things we learn over time—and the good news is that you can learn them, too. Whatever your age or situation, you can learn to overcome shyness or social awkwardness, banish loneliness, and enjoy strong, fulfilling friendships.

Here are a few questions you should answer before you continue reading…

Are shyness and insecurity a problem for you?

Are you afraid of looking stupid in social situations?

Do you worry a lot about what others think of you?

Do you frequently avoid social situations?

Do other people seem to have a lot more fun than you do in social situations?

Do you assume it's your fault when someone rejects you or seems uninterested?

Is it hard for you to approach people or join in conversations?

After spending time with others, do you tend to dwell on

and criticize your "performance?"

Do you often feel bad about yourself after socializing?

If you answered "yes" to these questions, this section of this ebook can help.

Tackling social insecurity and fear

When it comes to shyness and social awkwardness, the things we tell ourselves make a huge difference. Here are some common thinking patterns that can undermine your confidence and fuel social insecurity:

- Believing that you're boring, unlikeable, or weird.

- Believing that other people are evaluating and judging you in social situations.

- Believing that you'll be rejected and criticized if you make a social mistake.

- Believing that being rejected or socially embarrassed would be awful and devastating.

- Believing that what others think about you defines who you are.

If you believe these things, it's no wonder social situations seem terrifying.

People aren't thinking about you — at least not to the degree that you think. Most people are caught up in their own lives and concerns. Just like you're thinking about yourself and your own social concerns, other people are thinking about themselves. They're not spending their free time judging you. So stop wasting time worrying about what others think of you.

Many other people feel just as awkward and nervous as you do. When you're socially anxious, it can seem as though everyone else is an extrovert brimming with self-confidence. But that's not the case. Some people are better at hiding it than others, but there are many introverted people out there struggling with the same self-doubts as you are. The next person you speak to is just as likely to be worried about what you think of them!

People are much more tolerant than you think. In your mind, the very idea of doing or saying something embarrassing in public is horrifying. You're sure that everyone will judge you. But in reality, it's very unlikely that people are going to make a big deal over a social faux pas. Everyone has done it at some point so most will just ignore it and move on.

Learning to accept yourself

When you start realizing that people are NOT scrutinizing and judging your every word and deed, you'll automatically feel less nervous socially. But that still leaves the way you feel about yourself. All too often, we're our own worst critics. We're hard on ourselves in a way we'd never be to strangers—let alone the people we care about.

Learning to accept yourself doesn't happen overnight—it

requires changing your thinking.

You don't have to be perfect to be liked. In fact, our imperfections and quirks can be endearing. Even our weaknesses can bring us closer to others. When someone is honest and open about their vulnerabilities, it's a bonding experience—especially if they're able to laugh at themselves. If you can cheerfully accept your awkwardness and imperfections, you'll likely find that others will, too. They may even like you better for it!

It's okay to make mistakes. Everyone makes mistakes; it's part of being human. So give yourself a break when you mess up. Your value doesn't come from being perfect. If you find self-compassion difficult, try to look at your own mistakes as you would those of a friend. What would you tell your friend? Now follow your own advice.

Your negative self-evaluations don't necessarily reflect reality. In fact, they probably don't, especially if you:

- Call yourself names, such as "pathetic," "worthless," "stupid," etc.

- Beat yourself up with all the things you "should" or "shouldn't" have done.

- Make sweeping generalizations based on a specific event. For example, if something didn't go as planned, you tell yourself that you'll never get things right, you're a failure, or you always screw up.

When you're thinking such distorted thoughts, it's important to pause and consciously challenge them.

Pretend you're an impartial third-party observer, then ask yourself if there are other ways of viewing the situation.

Give up Shyness and Build social skills one step at a time

Giving up shyness to improve social skills requires practice. Just as you wouldn't expect to become good on the guitar without some effort, don't expect to become comfortable socially without putting in the time. That said, you can start small. Take baby steps towards being more confident and social, then build on those successes.

You should always:

- Smile at someone you pass on the street (No, you're not mad. Smiles….).

- Compliment someone you encounter during your day.

- Ask someone a casual question (at a restaurant, for example: "Have you been here before? How's the steak?")

- Start a conversation with a friendly cashier, receptionist, waiter, or salesperson.

How to face your biggest social fears

When it comes to the things that really scare us, you want to face your fears in a gradual way, starting with situations that are slightly stressful and building up to more anxiety-provoking scenarios. Think of it as a stepladder, with each rung a little more stressful than the last. Don't move on to the next step until you've had a positive experience with the step below. For example, if you're shy, and talking to new people at parties makes you extremely anxious, here is a stepladder you could use:

- Go to a party and smile at a few people.

- Go to a party and ask a simple question (e.g. "Do you know what time it is?"). Once they've answered, politely thank them and then excuse yourself. The key is to make the interaction short and sweet.

- Ask a friend to introduce you to someone at the party and help facilitate a short conversation.

- Pick someone at the party who seems friendly and approachable. Introduce yourself.

- Identify a non-intimidating group of people at the party and approach them. You don't need to make a big entrance. Just join the group and listen to the conversation. Make a comment or two if you'd like, but don't put too much pressure on yourself.

- Join another friendly, approachable group. This time, try to participate a bit more in the conversation.

More tips for Dealing with Shyness

- Fake it till you make it. Acting as if you're confident can make you feel more confident.

- Focus externally, not internally. Instead of worrying about how you're coming across or what you're going to say, switch your focus from yourself to the other person. You'll live more in the moment and you'll feel less self-conscious.

- Laugh at yourself. If you do something embarrassing, use humor to put things in perspective. Laugh, learn, and move on.

- Do things to help others or brighten another person's day. It can be something as small as a compliment or smile. When you spread positivity, you'll feel better about yourself.

Tips for Starting a Conversation with Someone New

Some people seem to instinctively know how to start a conversation with anyone, in any place. If you're not one of these lucky types, these tips will help you start talking when you first meet someone:

Here are some easy ways to engage in conversation with someone new:

- Remark on the surroundings or occasion. If you're at a party, for example, you could comment on the venue, the catering, or the music in a positive way. "I love this song," "The food's great. Have you tried the chicken?"

- Ask an open-ended question, one that requires more than just a yes or no answer. Adhere to the journalist's credo and ask a question that begins with one of the 5 W's (or 1 H): who, where, when, what, why, or how. For example, "Who do you know here?" "Where do you normally go on a Friday?" "When did you move here?" "What keeps you busy?" "Why did you decide to become a vegetarian?" "How is the wine?" Most people enjoy talking about themselves, so asking a question is a good way to get a conversation started.

- Use a compliment. For example, "I really like your purse, can I ask where you got it?" or "You look like you've done this before, can you tell me where I have to sign in?"

- Note anything you have in common and ask a follow-up question. "I play golf as well, what's your favorite local course?" "My daughter went to that school, too, how does your son like it?"

- Keep the conversation going with small talk. Don't say something that's obviously provocative and avoid heavy subjects such as politics or religion. Stick to light subjects like the weather, surroundings, and anything you have in common such as school, movies, or sports teams.

- Listen effectively. Listening is not the same as waiting for your turn to talk. You can't concentrate on what someone's saying if you're forming what you're going to say next. One of the keys to effective communication is to focus fully on the speaker and show interest in what's being said. Nod occasionally, smile at the person and make sure your posture is open and inviting. Encourage the speaker to continue with small verbal cues like "yes" or "uh huh."

What to do when you get tired of social situations

There's a common misconception that introverts aren't social. In fact, introverts can be just as social as extroverts. The difference between the two is that introverts lose energy when they're around people and recharge by spending time alone, while extroverts gain energy by spending time with other people.

What this means is that even socially confident introverts will feel tired after a lot of socializing. It doesn't mean there's anything wrong with you or that you're incapable of having a fulfilling social life. You just need to understand your limits and plan accordingly.

- Don't overcommit. It's okay to turn down social invitations because you need a break or schedule downtime after socializing. After a fun Saturday out with friends, for example, you may need to spend Sunday alone to rest and recharge.

- Take mini-breaks. There will be times when you're feeling drained, but you can't leave the situation for an extended alone time. Maybe you're at a busy work convention, you're on a getaway with friends, or you're visiting family for the holidays. In these circumstances, try to find time to slip away to a quiet corner when it wouldn't be seen as rude. Even 10 or 15 minutes here and there can make a big difference.

- Talk to your family and friends about your alone-time needs. Be upfront about the fact that socializing drains you. It's nothing to be ashamed about and trying to hide it will only add to your social exhaustion. Good friends will be sympathetic and willing to accommodate your needs.

Dealing with social setbacks and rejection

As you put yourself out there socially, there will be times when you feel judged or rejected. Maybe you reached out to someone, but they didn't seem interested in having a conversation or starting a friendship.

There's no question: rejection feels bad. But it's important to remember that it's part of life. Not everyone you approach will be receptive to starting a conversation, let alone becoming friends. Just like dating, meeting new people inevitably comes with some element of rejection. The following tips will help you have an easier time with social setbacks:

- Try not to take things too personally. The other person may be having a bad day, be distracted by other problems, or just not be in a talkative mood. Always remember that rejection has just as much to do with the other person as it does with you.

- Keep things in perspective. Someone else's opinion doesn't define you, and it doesn't mean that no one else will be interested in being your friend. Learn from the experience and try again.

- Don't dwell on mistakes. Even if you said something you regret, for example, it's unlikely that the other person will remember it after a short time. Stay positive; refrain from labeling yourself a failure, or from telling yourself that you'll never be able to make friends. The very shyest people do, and so will you.

Show Off Your Social Self

Yes, its time to show off your social self. So, set your shyness aside and let your social self shine through.

Although, we fear other people virtually as much as we fear spiders and snakes. Studies of anxiety disorders show that social phobia afflicts 55% percent of the world's population, right behind the fear of specific objects and situations. Short of having an officially diagnosable social phobia, though, occasional bouts of shyness can affect everyone. Without warning, you find yourself tongue-tied, afraid of making a public mistake or overwhelmed at the prospect of meeting new people. As a result, your stellar qualities are temporarily sent into hiding by your feelings of awkwardness and embarrassment.

The core of social phobia is the fear of embarrassment. People with this disorder have difficulty performing ordinary tasks in front of other people for fear of making a mistake or doing something that others perceive as foolish. Although you may think of social phobia like fear of public speaking, the actual disorder encompasses a much wider range of circumstances. In extreme forms, socially phobic avoid eating or drinking in public places. They don't want to be seen chewing, swallowing, or far worse, spilling food or liquids.

Although diagnosable conditions of social phobia involve complex disturbances in thoughts, emotions, and perhaps underlying physiology, ordinary shyness can range from occasional bouts of self-consciousness to a broader range of personality traits. When those bouts of self-consciousness strike you, there can be many possible causes.

One reason we fail to shine in a social situation is common egocentrism, the belief that other people are focused entirely on you and, hence, seeing your mistakes. The less confident you are about your abilities, the more likely it is we fear that the eyes on you will be critical. Simple conditioning can also make you hyper-sensitive. If an older relative or teacher constantly harped at you about your posture, for example, you may feel awkward about the way you walk now. Rather than put yourself out there in the bright light of the public eye, you go out of your way to avoid attention. You'll take the back stairs instead of striding through the center of the room to get from one end of a building to the other. If there's no other route available, you'll cling to the outer walls, hoping to melt into the shadows.

As difficult as physical shyness can be, verbal shyness can be even more disabling. It's hard to avoid attention in clutch situations in life in which you are expected to speak, such as a job or school admissions interview. A question is asked, and you are expected to answer. One-on-one social situations can also call for you to step out of your comfort zone. We've all had the stressful moments when we're sitting next to a virtual stranger at a meal or in a party and are expected to keep the conversational ball rolling. The classic scenario of meeting your loved one's friends or relatives for the first time can put anyone on edge, even the best talker in the world. Throw in a touch of shyness, and your anxiety can rapidly escalate.

Progress in the treatment of diagnosable social phobia is coming from the evidence-based treatments using cognitive-behavioral approaches. For example, a therapist can ask their clients to do "homework" in which they analyze the situations that cause them to be most fearful. Armed with the data, the therapists then work with the client to identify the so-called dysfunctional thoughts that crowd their mind and cause their inner panic to skyrocket. Once those thoughts are brought to the surface, the therapist works with the client to challenge and ultimately change them. One of the most critical steps in treating social phobia is overcoming the individual's social isolation. The new thoughts must be practiced in real-life settings for the treatment to work. Starting with small steps, the client can gradually experiment with the new thinking patterns, and feel better in a greater variety of previously threatening situations. Clients can also benefit from relaxation methods, mindfulness, and meditation in coping with the previously crippling feelings of social anxiety.

The same principles can be applied to helping people manage shyness, whether chronic or occasional. Unlike social phobia, ordinary shyness isn't a disabling condition, but it can be problematic when you need to make a favorable impression by what you say or do.

The first step to help you show off your social self is to

identify the situations in which your shyness reaches this problematic level and has actually prevented you from reaching the desired goal in life. We learn many of our dysfunctional social behaviors through old-fashioned classical conditioning. Just as you had to deal with the relative criticizing your posture, you may have to lurk in your memory a time when you blurted out a wrong answer to a question that cost you a desirable outcome. Having burned your chances by speaking too quickly, you naturally adapt by taking your time before you answer, or perhaps by saying nothing at all.

Even if you can't remember an exact moment in time when your shyness first took hold, you can nevertheless examine the thoughts going through your head when you've recently felt particularly shy. The chances are good that you felt unduly conscious of making a mistake of some kind or perhaps felt that you were being judged.

Now let's take those thoughts and challenge them. Are you actually being judged as harshly as you think you are? Did you really say or do something worthy of someone's eternal and scathing criticism? Or did you exaggerate its importance in your own mind? Even if the worst case scenario were true, and you did, in fact, offend someone else or say something that made you look bad, are you certain that it bothered the other person as much as it does you? Isn't it possible that the other person actually is willing to forgive you? If someone offended you and then apologized, wouldn't you be willing to consider accepting the apology? How about if someone else tripped in front of you, much to that person's dread? Would you really and truly judge that person as hopelessly clumsy for now and forever more?

You might well argue that this line of questioning is fine if someone already knows you, but what about the impression you make when you meet someone for the first time. Of course, first impressions are important. However, even if you mess up in your first moment of meeting someone by saying or doing something awkwardly, all is not lost. If we go with the "most people are forgiving" theory, it's even possible to make up for that glitch in the situation within milliseconds of its occurrence.

Now turn to the awkward pause in the conversation when you feel that the onus is on you to keep things going. Conversations are two-way streets, so if there's a lull, isn't it up to you to fill it? It's true, that person may be waiting for you to say something, or it might be expected that you do (as in an interview). In those particular situations, though, your job becomes slightly different. Turn down your internal monologue about how badly you're doing and instead focus on what is actually happening in the room. Don't listen to yourself, listen to the other person. Really pay attention to what he or she is asking, not on how miserable you're feeling or what you should say next. You got to that interview for a reason: you look good on paper, you had impressive recommendations, and you are the kind of person that they're looking for. This should help you build your confidence so that you stop worrying about how inadequate you must seem and instead be that person they expected to meet. Your social self will shine even in the toughest interview if you turn down that critical inner voice.

It's also important to recognize the benefits of shyness. Shy people may think that they're flawed when they compare themselves to their extraverted friends and family. However, think of your shyness as an asset. It takes a mix of personalities to make up a well-functioning social environment, whether it's a two-person couple, a large family, a classroom, or a work setting. Too many extroverts in a situation can lead to chaos. They clamor for attention and drown each other out. When something goes wrong, they let you know. You don't have to feel bad or ashamed of yourself just because you're not the noisiest person in the room. Shy people have the virtue of not being the squeaky wheel. Other people will appreciate you for who you are, not how loudly or frequently you make your presence known.

When it comes right down to it, challenging this negative view of yourself may ultimately be the most important step you can take to conquer your bouts with shyness. Accepting your personal qualities will help you focus more on enjoying social situations doing well in them, and giving yourself the confidence to do even better the next time you're in the spotlight.

Improve Your Conversations

HAVE YOU ever thought that some people are just natural conversationalists? No matter whom they're talking to, no matter the topic, they seem relaxed and comfortable. So you start to envy their skills— You want people to listen to you and ask you questions. All these are possible if you do all the things I'm going to talk about in this section. It will take some time, but gradually you will get to learn several different techniques for making a conversation more interesting.

The art of conversation, like any art, is a skill of elegance, nuance and creative execution.

I happen to believe that there is an art to everything we do and why not? Without flair and panache, most things become drudgery. Why settle for drudgery when you can have art?

When it comes to the art of conversation we've all met people who seem to have the knack for it. They can talk to anybody about anything and they seem to do it with complete ease. And while it's true that there are those who are born with the gift of gab, luckily for the rest of us, conversation skills can be developed and mastered.

In the previous chapter of this ebook, I gave some tips for starting a conversation - some easy ways to engage in conversation with someone new. Many of the same tips hold true for developing good conversational skills. Although I didn't really talk much about improving your conversation because we focused on Shyness. But in this section, I'll be going in depth. We'll be focusing on improving our conversation.

What Is Conversation?

A conversation is a form of communication; however, it is usually more spontaneous and less formal. We enter conversations for purposes of pleasant engagement in order to meet new people, to find out information and to enjoy social interactions.

While there is more to having good conversation skills than being a comedian, dramatic actor, or a great storyteller, it is not necessary to become more gregarious, animated, or outgoing. Instead, you can develop the ability to listen attentively, ask fitting questions, and pay attention to the answers - all qualities essential to the art of conversation. With diligent practice and several good pointers, anyone can improve their conversation skills.

<u>**Tips on How to Improve Your Conversation**</u>

1)Be a good listener. To some people, listening means planning what they are going to say when the other person stops talking. Real listening means focusing on what the other person is saying. One way to stay engaged is to respond to what they're saying: "What you've just said is interesting. Please tell me more about that." Or "Excuse me. Can you explain that again? I didn't quite get it."

Getting to know a new colleague, client, mentor, etc. can often be awkward if you're not confident in your conversation skills.

Luckily, you can practice those skills to be a better conversationalist, and one of the best ways to do that is through active listening.

I specifically say "active" listening here because it does require action to listen to someone in a way that allows you to respond thoughtfully. The most productive and meaningful conversations happen when both parties are aware of how to listen well.

Here are 8 steps to improve your conversation skills through active listening:

Step 1. Stop what you are doing

If you're going to engage in a conversation with someone, let them know you're listening intently by stopping what you're working on to give them your attention. If someone comes over to you and you don't make eye contact, continue working, and ask what they want, it'll be pretty clear you're not actually ready to listen.

Step 2. Shift your attention

When you're in the middle of something and someone comes over to talk to you, there are a few ways you can respond.

- Jot down a quick note as a reminder of where you left off, then shift your attention to the other person

- Ask them for a minute to finish writing a sentence or save a document and then turn to them to talk

- If you're pressed for time at the moment, ask if this is a quick conversation or if you can schedule a time later to talk

It's okay to let someone know that you're not available to talk right that second. Letting yourself finish a thought or scheduling a better time to talk will allow you to be more focused on the conversation, rather than continuing to think about what you were just doing or need to get done.

Step 3. Clear your mind

While you're shifting gears mentally to start a conversation, try to intentionally clear your mind. It's easy to let your mind wander to what you have to do next, or what's for dinner, or that great story you want to tell a friend, but right now it's time for the conversation at hand. Push those distracting thoughts aside and help yourself focus with the next step...

Step 4. Focus on the other person

Mentally focusing on someone's words is much easier when you are physically focused also. Turn away from your computer, face the person and make eye contact instead of constantly looking around the room. Giving them positive nonverbal signals that you're paying attention helps them to know that you're focused on the conversation.

Step 5. Listen

Alright, the time has come – time to listen.

Now that you're focused on the conversation, you need to maintain focus by actively listening to the other person. People speak at about 150 words per minute, but it's estimated that we think about 400-500 words per minute! That's a lot of extra space between their words and your thoughts to distract you. The next three steps are where you'll keep that space filled with thoughts relevant to the conversation rather than distractions.

Step 6. Write it down

If you hear something important or insightful that you don't want to forget, write it down! If you don't have a pen and paper and want to use your phone, just make sure to let the other person know you're making a note of something they said so they don't think you're ignoring them.

Step 7. Confirm what you heard

Sometimes what someone says doesn't come across the way they're thinking about it. If you're not sure you understand what they're saying (or even if you do), wait until they're done with a thought and then confirm what you took away from what they said.

This is one of those often skipped but highly important conversation skills since it helps the other person be more clear about their thoughts and prevents miscommunication.

Step 8. Process

There is more to Listening than just hearing.

Once you've gone through these steps to ensure you're truly listening to what someone has to say, you can process through it and formulate a response. One of the toughest aspects of listening well is not taking so much thought to respond that you miss what they're actually saying, but still have adequate time to think through what to say.

If you need more time to process, it's okay to tell them! Just make sure to confirm what they were trying to say, and let them know you'll think through it and respond soon.

Also, keep in mind that not every conversation needs a response to fix a problem. Sometimes a person just needs a listening ear but isn't looking for advice. If you're not sure whether to share your advice or not, again – ask!

2) Ensure there is a balance of giving and taking. A

conversation can get boring quickly if one person is doing all the talking while the other is trying to get a word in edgewise. When that happens whoever is not talking begins to tune out and there is no conversation!

There can be many reasons for a lack of giving and taking. Sometimes nervousness can get in the way and you ramble on without realizing it. Or, nervousness can make you freeze and you don't know what to say next. If you find yourself freezing up, take a deep breath and do your best to focus; smile, and then reflect on what you want to say. If the other person is the rambler and you've tried several times to interject but haven't been able to, then excuse yourself politely and move on.

If later on, you realize that you were the rambler, then at least you will have made the most important step towards improvement which is - awareness.

What you have to do is – Determine whether your tendency to dominate a conversation is due to nervousness or self-involvement.

Either way, review the conversation in your head. Look for spots where you could have paused and allowed the other person to talk. For future conversations, a good rule of thumb is after you make a point, pause for either agreement or an alternative point of view. Observe body language for cues whether to stop or continue. For example, is the person glossy-eyed and therefore bored? Are they moving towards you to speak and you just keep on talking? Are they looking elsewhere (for an escape) while you are carrying on? In a good conversation, each person needs to express themselves or it is no longer a conversation but a monologue.

3) Be interesting and have something to say. While you don't have to be a comedian, entertainer, or brilliant raconteur, you do need to be interesting otherwise what would you say? If you are not well informed, tend not to read much, or have very few interests, you will have very little to talk about except yourself. Unfortunately, no one wants to hear about your latest troubles, conquests, or daily routine. Yet so many dull conversationalists believe that's what people want to hear from them. Who hasn't been stuck with someone at a social event who blathers on about their family history, latest job interview, or the like?

To avoid being that person, become knowledgeable about world events, people in the news, or what's going on locally. Take time to keep up with the latest music, new technological discoveries, or recent best sellers. No one can know everything, so if you can enlighten someone during the course of a conversation, you'll be a hit! By the same token, you can learn something new as well.

Of course, not all conversations are knowledge sharing gatherings or discussions of global import. Many, especially at social functions, consist of light-hearted and cheerful banter. In such cases, be aware of the tone and mood of the conversation and go with the flow. If you are not particularly good at one-liners, or much of a jokester, you can always listen, smile and enjoy the humor. Never act as you feel out of place or ill at ease.

4) Be relaxed, be yourself. If you are on edge or trying to be someone you're not, it will show and therefore doom a conversation to failure before it starts. Admittedly, if you are not relaxed it's hard to appear as if you are. Slow down and take a deep breath. If you don't do your best to relax, you will end up saying something silly, unintelligible, or unrelated to the conversation. Also, smile warmly; it will make you appear pleasant and therefore, more approachable.

Note: if you are trying too hard to be something you're not, you will come across as a fake or a wannabe.

To start a conversation, go up to someone and introduce yourself. It is both polite and necessary to start things off smoothly. If the occasion calls for it, you can offer a handshake and then smile and make eye contact. Being friendly puts the other person at ease and opens the door for them to introduce themselves. If, for whatever reason, your attempt is not well-received and you notice the other person is cool or standoffish, bow out gracefully and move on. Do not take it as a rejection; merely consider that the person has their reasons for not reciprocating. Perhaps they are not feeling well, have had a bad day, or are not in the mood for conversation.

5) Use the best words. The ability to talk smoothly has a lot to do with choosing the precise words to convey your precise feelings or thoughts. Constantly develop your vocabulary and practice communicating as accurately as possible. It will help you develop a way with words and allow you to express yourself more easily.

6) To improve; practice and then practice some more. The art of conversation, like any skill, takes practice. Do not expect to be adept after your first few attempts. It will take practice as well as exposure to many different social situations. A good way to get practice before you venture out to an event is with family members and people you are comfortable with. They can give you helpful and supportive feedback, which in turn, gives you something to work on. You can never have too much practice!

Quick-Tips for The Art of Conversation

- Do not dominate a conversation or make it all about you. A monologue is not conversation.

- Show interest and curiosity in others.

- Strive for a balance of giving and taking.

- Be a good listener by maintaining good eye contact and asking pertinent questions.

- Train yourself to relax by using visualization, meditation, or other relaxation methods. Being relaxed is vital for good conversation.

- Do not interrupt and cut in with your own ideas before the other person is finished speaking.

- Maintain an open mind; everyone has a right to express themselves even if you don't agree with what they are saying.

- Although this is cliché, try to avoid topics such as sex, religion, and politics. You would be surprised at how many people get trapped by them and end up in verbal battle, not conversation.

- Be prepared by staying on top of the latest news, developments and world events.

- Be approachable by staying relaxed, smiling and maintaining a friendly attitude.

Possessing the art of conversation do not just improve your social skills, but also personal and work relationships. It gives you the opportunity to meet interesting new people and introduces you to various new topics and subject matter. With practice and application, anyone can improve their conversation skills.

Using Effective Conversation Skills to Influence Key Business Partners and Peers

Effective conversation skills are essential for achieving success. Beginning with active listening and continuing with clear correspondence, this strategy can maintain the respect necessary to influence your business partners and peers. It holds the power to motivate, stimulate creativity, and promote competitiveness to produce the best outcomes. The most successful people use a conversational style that is proactive, allowing them to work closely with others within their network and negotiate to achieve mutually beneficial goals.

Active listening allows multiple perspectives to be understood and creates a well-rounded view of the goals as well as the steps necessary to achieve them. Do not simply wait to speak. It's important to filter out the noise, read between the lines, and decipher what is truly important. Having an inquisitive nature and being willing to learn ensures that everyone is moving in the proper direction together.

To further ensure business partners and peers are on the same page, the conversation must continue in a thorough and efficient manner. This means being clear and concise while being assertive and confidently addressing all aspects of the discussion. Always say what you mean and mean what you say. When a potential roadblock is identified, courteously confront issues directly. By solving problems quickly, it is possible to produce immediate results with lasting positive outcomes.

Especially for internal conversation, honesty and realism can be key influencers. By maintaining a detailed, realistic understanding of the current situation, expectations of what needs to be completed, trust and confidence will be reinforced. Expressing the "why" and "how" (including measurable performance indicators) can help to motivate business partners and peers by illustrating success within reach.

It is critical to ask "why" and "how" when obtaining information in addition to facilitating it. Questions are the backbone of effective conversation because they offer clarity. Take ownership of your work and limitations – know when to ask for additional resources. There is no better way to get information from peers than to ask them for assistance.

While interacting with many people within a business setting, interpreting individual personality traits and approaching those people differently ensures effective conversation on a 1-to-1 level. For example, it is often necessary to actively open lines of conversation with people who don't speak up on their own. Some people respond better in an individual setting as opposed to a group. In any case, being respectful of everyone's time, energy, knowledge, and authority facilitate collaboration.

Even when faced with challenging situations, remaining level-headed and positive upholds high morale. Constructive criticism must embrace strengths to set others on a path to success. There are likely many ways to accomplish overarching goals and even more opinions about what is best. An effective team shares its knowledge and empowers each other to learn and understand new approaches. A mutually beneficial result can be reached while staying true to the strategic initiatives of each business partner and peer. Often, leveraging the team's existing strengths presents an opportunity to advocate for change and excel in a new realm.

From the subject matter to the audience receiving the information, a thorough understanding is necessary to communicate effectively. Strong interdepartmental collaboration and information delivery can help obtain success in all business aspects.

Why Having a Good Conversation Skill Is Important

For Instance; In your career, You may have all the necessary technical skills, the expertise and the experience that can really attest that you deserve that next promotion, but if you haven't got the conversation skills to back it up, you might miss the opportunity to level up in your career.

It is important to be able to have the conversation skills to communicate everything that will contribute for your career growth. You can't just silently plug away at your work without being open to opportunities for growth. You can actually make changes by means of using your conversation skills.

Conversation skills are important to any kinds of career because it is the base means with which you express yourself to other people, specifically your colleagues, your boss and other people you will deal with in the career you have chosen for yourself. Many competent graduates have missed out on opportunities for a rewarding career because they lacked the ample amount of conversation skills needed to be able to sustain the communication dynamics that come with every sort of promotion in work.

From the very beginning of your career, conversation skills are some sort of gauge with which other people measure your capability, coupled with your array of experiences and qualifications shown over a steady stream of performance for a set period of time. Conversation skills in itself will not land you the promotion or career growth you aspire, but a lack of it will certainly lessen your likelihood of bagging a good job, especially if they have seen better conversationalists among your colleagues who may be aspiring for the same career growth form that you want.

Having good conversation skills does not only give a good edge compared to your colleagues, but it will also help you gain the general goodwill of most people in your workplace. If you are as gracious with your words as you are excellent with your work, people will just naturally trust you and establish you as someone who is reliable and fun to work with. Good conversation skills ease the gaps that come between people who have little or almost nothing in common.

Not all career growth opportunities are easily bestowed. You might find your efforts less visible to the people who can help you land that promotion. In this case, you will definitely need to be backed up by your subtle and well-thought out conversation skill strategies that will help you be able to express yourself and assert your qualification to your bosses without making them feel threatened or imposed upon.

Conversation skills do not only deal with the fluent pronunciation, the good articulation or the well-versed array of words. Veering from the technical aspect is the emotional correspondence which makes your eloquent speaking capabilities more felt by those who will hear you and converse with you. Body language is also a great factor which will either make or break your statements (We'll also be looking at Body Language in this book). A good investment as you grow in your career is to enhance or refresh your conversation skills. All the information put together in this section is what you need to Improve, as well as enhance and refresh your conversation skill.

If you are a person with good conversation skills, you also naturally inspire others to do the same thing even without trying. Good conversation skills are not just admirable, it is also contagious especially with people you interact with on a regular basis. If you are a catalyst to having good conversation skills at work, you can also expect your colleagues and consequently, your entire company, to grow well with you in that arena. Having good conversation skills is like shining a flashlight on what is otherwise considered as a typical work routine day. In addition to that, if you have cultivated yourself to attain good conversation skills, you will definitely reap what you sow by means of meeting more interesting people who can match your conversation skills and double your growth, professionally as well as personally.

Build Genuine Relationships

This is a one size fits all guide to building the right kind of relationship.

How many of us have learned how to build genuine relationships? Where did we learn? At home? At school? There are art and science to building genuine relationships.

In this section, I want to give you some practical tips on how you can build genuine relationships — the kinds of relationships that cannot be scaled.

7 Tips for Building Genuine Relationships

Here are 7 tips on how you can build genuine, sincere relationships:

1. Create a safe environment where you can trust and share openly without fear.

Don't interrupt, even if you need to put your hand over your mouth to stop yourself. Learn to fight fairly. No name calling. Don't make threats. Apologize when you know you should. If you're too angry to really listen, stop! Go into another room, take space for yourself, breathe, and calm down.

2. Talk to Everyone

A great way to build genuine relationships is by making an effort to talk to as many people as you can.

Making an effort to talk to more random strangers will actually bring you more feelings of happiness, in spite of widespread notions that you would be happier keeping to yourselves. Similarly, making an effort to talk to more people can also help you to build more genuine relationships.

A simple "Hello" or "How are you?" may be all it takes to get a conversation started, and then you are off to the races. You never know who you might be in line with at the grocery store or at a department store, especially during the holidays, when more people venture out of their homes. You can strike up a conversation and create a brand new relationship.

3. Separate the facts from the feelings.

What beliefs and feelings get triggered in you during conflicts? Ask yourself: Is there something from my past that is influencing how I'm seeing the situation now? The critical questions you want to ask: Is this about him or her, or is it really about me? What's the real truth?

Once you're able to differentiate facts from feelings, you'll see your partner more clearly and be able to resolve conflicts from clarity.

4. Develop compassion.

Practice observing yourself and your partner without judging. Part of you might judge, but you don't have to identify with it. Judging closes a door. The opposite of judging is compassion. When you are compassionate, you are open, connected, and more available to dialoguing respectfully with your partner. As you increasingly learn to see your partner compassionately, you will have more power to choose your response rather than just reacting.

5. Make time for your relationship.

No matter who you are or what your work is, you need to nurture your relationship. Make sure you schedule time for the well-being of your relationship. That includes "hanging out" and also taking downtime together. Frequently create a sacred space together by shutting off all things technological and digital. Like a garden, the more you tend to your relationship, the more it will grow.

6. Take Extraordinary Measures to Delight the People You Meet

You should learn to take extraordinary measures not just to acquire users, but also to make them happy. This advice can apply not just to start-up businesses, but to the people you come across as well — you should take extraordinary measures to not just acquire friends, but also to make them happy.

As an example, a company that helps people to build online forms. When it was just starting out, someone at the company just sends each new user a hand-written thank you note. Can you imagine the impression that made on their early adopters?

What if we all took this approach to life? What if we all tried to delight the people we meet?

You may be chortling under your breath at this suggestion (I can hear you.) But why not? In my experience, it doesn't take much to delight people, because the bar is generally set pretty low. For example, you could dash off a quick, hand-written note to the next person you meet, or maybe to some guy who wrote a super helpful guest post you just read (hint hint). You may just create a friend and an advocate for life.

7. Take a Genuine Interest in Others

At the core of building relationships in a genuine way is taking interest in the people you meet. And taking interest in a person is, by definition, a genuine activity. It requires that you drill down and devote your solitary attention to one person.

If you want to make sure your interests are perceived as genuine, then focus on the following:

- Listen intently and ask good questions. Be completely present with the person, by putting away your phone, making eye contact, listening to what they have to say, and asking good questions. Nothing builds rapport more than being curious about the other person.

- Focus on the details. Remember details about the people you meet, such as their hobbies, their children's names, or their hometown. Don't expect to keep all of these details in your head. Personally, I write them down using my dairy, but you could do it whatever way works for you.

- Remember names. Here's another detail you don't want to forget: the person's name! Remembering people's names is a fast way to build trust.

- Follow up. Following up with people demonstrates your interest in them was genuine and sincere, and not limited to when they are in front of you. Follow up by sending the person you've met invitations to special events, by making helpful introductions, or by sharing resources or relevant information. For example, if I had a conversation where I recommended a great coffee company, I might follow up with an email including a link to the coffee company.

How Being an Interesting Person Can Help You Build Genuine Relationships

Are You an Interesting Person?

In our culture today much emphasis is placed on looks, sex appeal and being youthful. Many individuals spend a disproportionate amount of time working on their outer packages.

Rather than being introspective, they go to great lengths to be fashionable and trendy as well as making sure they are seen at the latest "in" places.

Sadly, when little or no effort is being made to develop the intellect or an interesting personality, many good-looking young men and women come across as being flighty and uninformed, as well as self-centered and self-absorbed.

Evidence of this unhealthy trend can be witnessed in the behavior of some of today's young celebrities and pop stars who often serve as role models (whether we like it or not) for our children.

We are bombarded daily with news of their antics where they engage in self-indulgent and often irresponsible behavior. Some of them end up in a rehab which quite often doesn't address the real problem.

Although physical attraction is very helpful in the preservation of our species, evolution has come a long way in giving us more than solely our appearance to attract each other.

For a solid, meaningful relationship to develop between two parties they must have more to contribute to each other beyond their initial physical attraction.

When two people have little in common except for their good looks, there is virtually no place for a relationship to go. Instead, they must enjoy each other as individuals and be able to develop a bond or friendship. There must be substance, shared interests, willingness to grow, and mutual respect.

So what is the answer?

Become someone whose company others seek. Have something meaningful to contribute. Not only will you enrich your own life in the process, but you will also enrich the lives of others. Short and Simple!

Here are some ways you can become an interesting person:

- Cultivate a variety of interests
- Expand your knowledge in the arts, music, literature, sports
- Take a genuine interest in others
- Read more
- Stay on top of current events
- Express your informed opinions
- Become a good conversationalist
- Be aware
- Develop and appreciate humor
- Develop good conversation skills
- Be self-confident

Moreover, developing all aspects of your self - your mind, body, intellect, and spirit. It's never too late to start!

Building Genuine Relationships for Business

Customer relationships are one of the most important parts of your business, if not the most important. So, how do you begin building those Genuine, meaningful, and lifelong relationships with customers?

We are writers, entrepreneurs, bloggers, influencers, people, and humans. At our core, we are people that want others to do business with us, to get our name out there. But from well-established businesses to the small start-up, there is one thing that we need to be doing to truly grow; which is having genuine relationships. To sit down and actually have good conversations with your potential or existing customers.

Customer relationship building starts before someone even makes a purchase. In this section, I have laid out tips that will help you to build Genuine relationships with your clients/customers successfully.

Building a genuine relationship is undoubtedly a struggle for a lot of people for a variety of reasons even outside of work. So it's to be expected businesses to run into the same sort of problems. We are people behind the business at the end of the day.

You can start fixing a lot of those issues by doing the following things listed below:

- Engage with a person, ask questions

As a business person, you should learn to ask your customers/clients questions. Not necessarily about what it is they do because sometimes they seem boring and unnecessary. Instead, ask about why they followed you on social media. What got them to be a consumer of your product or service?

Understanding a person's reasoning can be meaningful once you grow a massive audience. Also questions in general help in getting an idea of the person as well.

Asking questions shows you are interested, that you actually care.

- Ask about passions or hobbies

Yes, it is necessary for you to know about the passions or hobbies of your customers or potential clients. Not necessarily to build up more of a demographic but you can understand what people are passionate about. When you are an author like myself, your brand is you. In my case, I'm the only employee for myself so it's important for me to get along with other people.

- Show your authenticity

Some of these tactics can be difficult if you have more people involved in a business. However, there are more creative ways to show authenticity to others. For someone flying solo, it's a matter of being personal.

I take pride in showing off my changes, what I'm up to, and inspiring people in my own way. Businesses can do the same by showing behind the scenes stuff, asking for suggestions and so on. This helps you build and maintain genuine relationships with your customers.

- Be Responsive and Personal

Timely and efficient communication is absolutely imperative as a business owner. Being available to clients is key to letting them know their business and satisfaction are important to you. Make sure you are responding to their phone calls and emails professionally and in a timely manner.

Although you want to be efficient, making the time to connect with clients is a core element of building genuine relationships with them. Make it a point to get to know them, whether that is asking them about their family vacation they just went on or how their new puppy is doing. Of course, your product or service is always the number one focus, but it is important for you to let your clients know that you acknowledge them and see them as a person, more than solely a business asset.

- Share Knowledge

Chances are your company is filled with a number of amazing services or products. If your client doesn't understand your area of expertise, they may feel intimidated about the intricacies of your business, and therefore disconnected. This is an opportunity to share information.

Helping your client understand what your business is all about will build trust and confidence in the process. Explaining to the client what you do, why you do it, and how you make decisions will help them feel more comfortable with you as a business partner. You can even add in your own story of why you got started in this industry and how you've seen your business grow to give it a personal touch.

- Be Open to Feedback

Be grateful for the feedback received from clients; both good and not so good. It may be difficult to hear feedback that you may not have been anticipating. Be open to receiving these comments and see if there are any aspects of your business that could be improved.

There may be an issue in your firm you were blind to before a customer brought it up. Thank them for sharing their thoughts with you and work to solve any problems they are experiencing in a kind, thoughtful way. This will go a long way in building a genuine relationship with that client. This will also help in building trust and credibility with your clients.

- Set Realistic Expectations

Consider the famous quote, "Under-promise and over-deliver." This is essential to remember when working with clients. Overestimate deadlines so that when your team finishes a project before the deadline, your client will be nothing short of thrilled. One of the most detrimental things to your relationship with a client is to overcommit and under-deliver.

Building trust in an untrusting world is essential. Once your clients trust you, they become loyal to you. And, loyal customers are your best referrals!

Get Started Building Your Genuine Relationships

Now it's time for you to get started. Take the advice above and begin building genuine relationships, whether at work, school, or home, etc. Don't worry if your system is not perfect. Don't think about optimization or making sure you are maximizing your efficiency.

It doesn't matter so much where you begin or where you end up, but just that you get started. You have to start somewhere. Just take it one relationship at a time.

Body Language

What Is Body Language?

Body language is a non-verbal form of communication using physical movements and behaviors rather than words. The expressions and postures used in body language can be used to understand how others feel about a situation and the people involved. Facial expressions and posture are both considered body language, recognizing these expressions and postures as a cue to how someone feels can change the whole dynamic of a situation.

When someone smiles, everyone recognizes it as a welcoming, happy expression, but what if that person smiles to be polite but they are not happy about the situation? Reading body language involves more than an obvious facial expression, how that person is standing about others in the conversation, their posture, and their eyes can tell you more about that smile.

Many body language cues are not conscious, slight changes in facial expressions and posture can be telling about how someone feels, and they may not even realize they are giving away their thoughts. The tone of someone's voice and involuntary muscle movements are also considered body language; detectives even use knowledge of these involuntary language cues to help them read situations and people during investigations.

Relationships are built on communication. I share with you, and you share with me. When we share with each other, we understand each other better, which grows our relationship deeper.

The tricky part is that a lot of conversation is non-verbal. I might not use words to tell you if I feel upset with you, but I will physically draw back from you---for instance, by crossing my arms, angling my feet towards the door, or avoiding eye contact. If you don't catch my physical signals, you might not realize that something is wrong until it's too late.

Even if you understand the body language signals other people are sending, you might not realize what your own body is communicating. When your body language is cold and standoffish, people are unlikely to approach you, even if you want them to.

Fortunately, it's easy to make body language a positive part of your interactions. In this section, I will walk you through the simple, practical principles that will guide you to a great interpretation of body language and how you can improve your Social skills with them.

Here's what to look for when you're trying to interpret body language.

- Facial Expressions

Think for a moment about how much a person is able to convey with just a facial expression. A smile can indicate approval or happiness. A frown can signal disapproval or unhappiness. In some cases, our facial expressions may reveal our true feelings about a particular situation. While you say that you are feeling fine, the look on your face may tell people otherwise.

Just a few examples of emotions that can be expressed via facial expressions include:

- Happiness
- Sadness
- Anger
- Surprise
- Disgust
- Fear
- Confusion
- Excitement
- Desire
- Contempt

The expression on a person's face can even help determine if we trust or believe what the individual is saying. One study found that the most trustworthy facial expression involved a slight raise of the eyebrows and a slight smile. This expression, the researchers suggested, conveys both friendliness and confidence.

Facial expressions are also among the most universal forms of body language. The expressions used to convey fear, anger, sadness, and happiness are similar throughout the world.

Research even suggests that we make judgments about people's intelligence based on their faces and expressions. One study found that individuals who had narrower faces and more prominent noses were more likely to be perceived as intelligent. People with smiling, joyful expression were also judged as being more intelligent than those with angry expressions.

- The Eyes

The eyes are frequently referred to as the "windows to the soul" since they are capable of revealing a great deal about what a person is feeling or thinking. As you engage in conversation with another person, taking note of eye movements is a natural and important part of the communication process. Some common things you may notice include whether people are making direct eye contact or averting their gaze, how much they are blinking, or if their pupils are dilated.

When evaluating body language, pay attention to the following eye signals:

Eye gaze: When a person looks directly into your eyes while having a conversation, it indicates that they are interested in and paying attention. However, prolonged eye contact can feel threatening. On the other hand, breaking eye contact and frequently looking away might indicate that the person is distracted, uncomfortable, or trying to conceal his or her real feelings.

Blinking: Blinking is natural, but you should also pay attention to whether a person is blinking too much or too little. People often blink more rapidly when they are feeling distressed or uncomfortable. Infrequent blinking may indicate that a person is intentionally trying to control his or her eye movements. For example, a poker player might blink less frequently because he is purposely trying to appear unexcited about the hand he was dealt with.

Pupil size: Pupil size can be a very subtle nonverbal communication signal. While light levels in the environment control pupil dilation, sometimes emotions can also cause small changes in pupil size. For example, you may have heard the phrase "bedroom eyes" used to describe the look someone gives when they are attracted to another person. Highly dilated eyes, for example, can indicate that a person is interested or even aroused.

- The Mouth

Mouth expressions and movements can also be essential in reading body language. For example, chewing on the bottom lip may indicate that the individual is experiencing feelings of worry, fear, or insecurity.

Covering the mouth may be an effort to be polite if the person is yawning or coughing, but it may also be an attempt to cover up a frown of disapproval. Smiling is perhaps one of the greatest body language signals, but smiles can also be interpreted in many ways. A smile may be genuine, or it may be used to express false happiness, sarcasm, or even cynicism.

When evaluating body language, pay attention to the following mouth and lip signals:

Pursed lips: Tightening the lips might be an indicator of distaste, disapproval, or distrust.

Lip biting: People sometimes bite their lips when they are worried, anxious, or stressed.

Covering the mouth: When people want to hide an emotional reaction, they might cover their mouths in order to avoid displaying smiles or smirks.

Turned up or down: Slight changes in the mouth can also be subtle indicators of what a person is feeling. When the mouth is slightly turned up, it might mean that the person is feeling happy or optimistic. On the other hand, a slightly down-turned mouth can be an indicator of sadness, disapproval, or even an outright grimace.

- The Arms and Legs

The arms and legs can also be useful in conveying nonverbal information. Crossing the arms can indicate defensiveness. Crossing legs away from another person may indicate dislike or discomfort with that individual.

Other subtle signals such as expanding the arms widely may be an attempt to seem larger or more commanding while keeping the arms close to the body may be an effort to minimize oneself or withdraw from attention.

When you are evaluating body language, pay attention to some of the following signals that the arms and legs may convey:

- Crossed arms might indicate that a person feels defensive, self-protective, or closed-off.

- Standing with hands placed on the hips can be an indication that a person is ready and in control, or it can also possibly be a sign of aggressiveness.

- Clasping the hands behind the back might indicate that a person is feeling bored, anxious, or even angry.

- Rapidly tapping fingers or fidgeting can be a sign that a person is bored, impatient, or frustrated.

- Crossed legs can indicate that a person is feeling closed off or in need of privacy.

- Posture

How we hold our bodies can also serve as an important part of body language. The term posture refers to how we hold our bodies as well as the overall physical form of an individual. Posture can convey a wealth of information about how a person is feeling as well as hints about personality characteristics, such as whether a person is confident, open, or submissive.

Sitting up straight, for example, may indicate that a person is focused and paying attention to what's going on. Sitting with the body hunched forward, on the other hand, can imply that the person is bored or indifferent.

When you are trying to read body language, try to notice some of the signals that a person's posture can send.

- Open posture involves keeping the trunk of the body open and exposed. This type of posture indicates friendliness, openness, and willingness.

- Closed posture involves hiding the trunk of the body often by hunching forward and keeping the arms and legs crossed. This type of posture can be an indicator of hostility, unfriendliness, and anxiety.

Now you know how to interpret body language, let's look at how you can improve your Social skills with the body language tips below.

Improve Your Social Skills with These 10 Body Language Tips

For every occasion, there's always this one individual who seems to captivate everyone. Her smile lights up the room, people gather to talk to her, and you can't help but be drawn to her. She may not be the prettiest person at the event, but something about her feels exciting and inviting.

Who is she? How is she able to appear so likable to both men and women?

The answer is not in her choice of clothing or her witty remarks (although those are important, too). Her allure comes from her body language. Want to capture the audience the next time you walk into a party? Practice these 10 tips and you'll be on your way to improving your Social skills.

1. Have an open and relaxed posture.

Whether you're standing, sitting, or walking, having the right posture not only makes you look charming, it also helps you to appear taller. If you've been slouching for a long time, there are plenty of easy exercises to fix your stance. It also helps to observe yourself using a full-length mirror. Sit, walk, and stand in front of it for about 5-10 minutes each day until you have the correct posture. This means:

- Head straight and relaxed
- Shoulders back
- Abdomen in
- Knees slightly bent

Once you have mastered good posture, you'll find that you feel more comfortable and confident when facing people.

2. Smile with your eyes.

Your smile is one of your most potent weapons to make you likable instantly. A genuine smile is supposed to reach your eyes, creating tiny crinkles that light up your face. This suggests that you are truly happy, and nothing is more attractive than a person who smiles as they mean it. According to research, smiling also alleviates stress and can influence your level of success.

Believe it or not, you can enhance your smile simply by practicing it every day! Face a mirror, take a deep breath, hold it, and slowly exhale before smiling. You'll notice that you feel more relaxed and your smile looks genuine. Try this a couple more times until you feel confident!

3. Subtly mirror tiny movements.

Mirroring is a body language technique that successful people use to gain rapport. When done right, it should make you more likable without much effort. It's part of our psychology to respond positively to individuals who are like us. In fact, a baby's body functions (like its heartbeat) sync with the mother even before birth.

Good mirroring begins by first observing the other person's movements. Is he leaning forward? Crossing his legs? Nodding? Reflect these actions with your own body to quickly develop a bond of trust. This method has been proven numerous times in different experiments. So at your next party, watch people closely. Mirror their movements to connect better with any person in the room.

4. Use a quick touch on the forearm or shoulder.

Don't underestimate the power of a quick pat on the back or a friendly touch on the arm. Unlike words, these are universally understood and can convey more meaning. For example, if you really like a person, you may lightly touch their arm during a conversation. Similar to mirroring, this builds rapport with the people you meet. Remember not to overdo this though! Just a light tap is enough — never linger!

5. Maintain good eye contact.

There's no doubt that making eye contact is one of the most

powerful body language arsenals. However, doing it wrong will make you look creepy. Combine this with tip #2: smile while making eye contact to make yourself irresistible instantly. Ten seconds is a safe time limit before looking elsewhere. Otherwise, you will trigger a person's defense mechanism and make them feel uncomfortable.

6. Turn your body towards the person.

Also known as the "big baby pivot," this involves turning your entire body towards another person. This body language trick got its name from the way most folks turn their attention to a baby. When being introduced to someone, make sure to give your undivided attention by pivoting your body towards them. This delivers the message that they're special and you're interested in them. True interest in another person makes you super sociable in return!

7. Use open hand gestures.

The handshake that we practice today is, in fact, an early custom to prove that you're not hiding any weapons. That's why we have suspicions when people don't show their hands. With this in mind, use gestures to make you the most Sociable person in the room.

When conversing or speaking to a crowd, use certain hand gestures to create an impact. Here are a few:

- Use your fingers when listing points
- A solid fist means you're determined

- Make a sweeping motion to mean "everything"

- Bring hands to your chest when talking about a personal experience

Consider your audience when using hand gestures.

Note: one sign could mean a world of difference in another culture, so use with caution!

8. Pause for a few seconds.

This is a subtle yet very effective part of your body language. You can implement quick pauses during conversations or speeches when:

- You're asked a difficult or personal question (this gives you enough time to think of a good answer)

- You want to build a dramatic effect (pausing between statements is a sign that you're about to deliver big news)

- You want to create an air of mystery (particularly when coupled with a small smile)

Pausing is also great when used just before you smile. It shows that you're not someone who gives it away so easily.

9. Nod to show confidence in opinion.

According to one study, nodding doesn't necessarily mean that you agree with something. Rather, this simple action strengthens an already existing opinion. In a gathering, for instance, nodding your head to the speaker reinforces whatever he or she is saying. This creates a connection between you two — even if you don't really agree with everything they say. It's also a sign that shows you're paying attention.

10. Avoid fidgeting.

Feeling nervous during an important event? Need to calm your nerves before meeting with clients? If you want to be instantly sociable, one of the things you should avoid is looking restless. If you have the habit of fiddling with your fingers when worried, it could signal to others that you're insecure. Project an appealing aura by standing tall yet relaxed.

If you're still feeling anxious, be sure to bring something familiar with you, like your favorite pen or necklace. These are usually called "comfort objects." According to experts, carrying something you associate with good memories will help reduce anxiety. Look at it or hold it in your hand for a few seconds to remind you that everything's going to be okay. Then, proceed to be your best, irresistible, sociable self!

When Your Body Language and Your Words Don't Agree

Unfortunately, most people don't think about their own body language. They might spend a lot of time thinking of the perfect words to say, but never realize that their body language and their words are sending very different messages.

For example, say you have had a long, hard day, but your friend wants to talk with you about something that they are struggling with. You obviously care about your friend, so you tell them that you want to talk.

But if during the conversation you are yawning, looking at the clock, and leaning back in your chair with your arms crossed, your friend might conclude that you don't really want to talk with them after all. They storm off, and you are left wondering what you said wrong. (Of course, you didn't say anything wrong---that's the point!)

That's just one example; it's easy to think of other ways your own body language can create misunderstandings. When your words and your body are sending different messages, people will tend to go with the message that your body is sending. If you didn't mean to send that message, trouble ensues.

The Power of Self-Awareness

Fortunately, that trouble is entirely avoidable. Just be aware of the messages your body is sending. Your body is going to communicate---that's just part of being human. Take the time to notice what it is communicating, and you can make sure that your body and your words are sending the same message.

Let me be clear. I'm not talking about changing your body language to mask deception---if your words are communicating something untrue, then you should change your words instead of your body language. Relationships built on deception will never give you the long-term satisfaction and intimacy that you need.

Instead, focus on presenting a cohesive, genuine message of the thing that is both true and most important. If you are tired but you care about your friend, the message that is most important is "I care about you" not "I'm tired" (even though both messages are true.) If you are excited to meet someone new but also nervous, the message that is most important is "I am excited to meet you" not "I am nervous."

The message of "I care about you" is more important than the message of "I am very tired", because your commitment to your friend runs deeper than your physical fatigue. The message of "I am excited to meet you" is more important than the message of "I'm feeling nervous" because your desire to make a new friend is greater than your nervousness.

It's okay to make sure your body language communicates the message that is most important. That's not deception; just making sure the most important message is communicated well. When you are aware of your own body language, it allows you to be sure that both your words and your body language reflect the message that is most true.

So take the time to be aware of your own body language. The lists of comfort and discomfort signals are just as useful when you are using them to understand your own body language. Be aware of what your body is communicating, and make the effort to mute discomfort signals and broadcast comfort signals. You'll find that as you match your body language to your words, you will have much greater success in your interactions.

Practicing and Using Body Language to Better Your Social Skills

The best way to practice body language is to mimic the posture, gesture, and facial expression in a full-length mirror. Using a mirror will help you control your body language and use it to express what you want, when you want. This practice technique will help you recognize body language cues from others as well as recognize your postures, gestures and facial expressions.

You can practice micro expressions in a mirror too. If you practice making them enough, you will eventually be able to recognize them in others. You can also look up images of micro-expressions on the internet and use them to help you recognize them.

You will not be able to control micro-expressions, but you can learn to control your posture, gestures and facial expressions. Mastering body language will help you eliminate any unwanted postures, expressions or gestures from ruining your first impression or interfering in social situations. You can use body language to put people at ease during meetings, appear interested and curious when conversations get boring, and generally improve your social interactions in all situations.

Everyone can benefit from learning to read body language. Reading body language can help you save social interactions that are becoming awkward, or boring. This skill can also help you improve your social skills by recognizing body language cues that show someone is ready to leave, in a hurry, un-interested, or intimidated. The more you know, the easier it is to use this skill; eventually it will become second nature and your social skills will improve naturally.

Stop Procrastinating

Why so many people procrastinate and how it can be overcome

For most people, procrastination, irrespective of what they say, is not about being lazy. In fact, for them, when they procrastinate they often work intensely for long stretches just before their deadlines. Working long and hard is the opposite of lazy, so that can't be the reason we do it. So, why do we procrastinate and, more importantly, what can we do about it?

As suggested above, some say they procrastinate because they are lazy. Others claim they "do better" when they procrastinate. I encourage you to be critical and reflective of these explanations. Virtually everyone who says this habitually procrastinates and has not completed an important academic task or has not reached out to that person they want to be friends with which they planned to.

If you pretty much always procrastinate, and never really approach your wants, then you can't accurately say that you know you do better. Still other people say they like the rush of leaving things to the end and meeting a deadline. But they usually say this when they are NOT working under that deadline. They say this works before or after cramming when they have forgotten the negative consequences of procrastinating such as feelings of anxiety and stress, fatigue, and disappointment from falling below their own standards and having to put their life on hold for chunks of time. Not to mention, leaving things to the end dramatically increases the chances something will go wrong - like getting sick or a computer problem - and you not being able to socialize with people you ought to. So, procrastination can be hard on us and actually increase our chances of failing, but we do it anyway. How come?

Also, when it comes to socializing, procrastination is not a matter, solely, of having poor social skills, either, but rather can be traced to underlying and more complex psychological reasons. For example, if you procrastinate, then you always have the excuse of not going to events you planned to, so your sense of your ability is never threatened.

Procrastination also affects students. For example, In school, when there is so much pressure on getting a good grade on, say, a paper, it's no wonder that students want to avoid it and so put off their work. For the most part, our reasons for delaying and avoiding are rooted in fear and anxiety about doing poorly, of doing too well, of losing control, of looking stupid, of having one's sense of self or self-concept challenged. We avoid doing things to avoid our abilities being judged. And, if we happened to succeed, we feel that much "smarter.". So, what can we do to overcome our tendencies to procrastinate?

Now, before I show you the EXACT steps you can take to demolish procrastination. First, you need to have an understanding of the REASONS WHY you procrastinate and the function procrastination serves in your life. You can't come up with an effective solution if you don't really understand the root of the problem. As with most problems, awareness and self-knowledge are the keys to figuring out how to stop procrastinating. For a lot of people acquiring this insight about how procrastination protects them from feeling like they are not able enough, and keeping it in mind when they are tempted to fall into familiar, unproductive, procrastinating habits goes a long way to solving the problem.

How to stop procrastinating in 5 steps

In this section, I want to show you how to stop procrastinating in 5 simple steps. You need to stop waiting for motivation to strike and take action today.

Step 1: Be brutally honest about your priorities

How often has someone asked you to do something and you told them, "I don't have enough time for that right now."

For example:

FRIEND: Hey, do you want to check out that new bar tonight?

YOU: Sorry, I'm super busy tonight. Maybe some other time. (Proceed to stay at home, binge-watching Netflix all night.)

Another example:

FRIEND: I'm going to take that improv class you said you were interested in. Want to join?

YOU: Ugh sorry, I don't have enough time right now.

We LOVE using "time" as an excuse because it's easy. Who is going to accuse you of having too much time on your hands? Nobody.

When we make this excuse, however, we only cheat ourselves and we kill our social skill.

Instead, it's better to be honest with yourself and others and say, "I appreciate the offer, but that's just not a priority for me right now." Doing this forces you to confront the lies you often tell yourself — and helps you recognize what is important to you … and what isn't.

Plus, who would you admire more? The person who says, "I don't have enough time" and doesn't show up to anything, or the person who tells you, "I appreciate the offer but that's just not one of my priorities right now?"

Of course, it's the person who is honest with you.

Once you start recognizing what is NOT a priority, you'll start recognizing things that ARE.

ACTION STEP: Be honest and evaluate your priorities.

To help you evaluate what is a priority for you, I highly recommend what I call an "honesty bath."

To do this, keep track of the goals you make for this month. Record them with a Word doc, pen and paper, Excel, whatever. Then put them in a drawer and set a calendar alert for the last day of the month.

At the end of the month, go through the list and see which ones you actually accomplished and which ones you didn't get to. Then decide whether you're going to:

Delete

Defer

Do it

If you say that you're going to say "Hi" to someone in your school, but whenever you see the person coming your way, you just look away and pass …you're NOT going to talk to that person.

Delete.

If you claim you're going to stay back and attend your youth meeting in church with your fellow youths every Sunday after service, and you haven't done that in a month after saying "You will", guess what? You're NOT going to stay back for that meeting.

Defer.

Are you actually headed to the gym 3x/week with your colleagues like you said you would? Keep DOING IT.

This takes a lot of self-awareness and determination because you have to be ruthlessly honest about your strengths and weaknesses. But by looking at your past behavior, you can drastically change your future behavior for the better.

The best part? It stops that low-level anxiety we all get from having a bunch of goals bouncing around in our head. Once you make the decision, you can live guilt-free and use your energy to commit to things you'll actually do.

Step 2: Stop feeling guilty

It's interesting how people fall into the paradox of guilt — and don't even realize it's happening.

How often have you talked to a friend about working out, partying, or socializing with people in school, and heard them say something like, "Yeah, I know I really should be doing that but…" followed by some lame excuse as to why they're procrastinating on something important?

"I know I really should be doing that" is just code for "I'm not going to do that at all."

It's the same with people in credit card debt — many don't even know how much debt they have! They'd rather avoid their statements and bury their head in the sand than face the reality of how much they owe.

Why does this happen? Guilt. Plain and simple. It's the reason why we brush things off with meaningless excuses and run away from the actual issue.

If you truly want to stop procrastinating and improve your

social skills, as well as become a productivity machine, you need to hold yourself accountable.

ACTION STEP: Don't run away from your guilt.

When you do feel guilty, take these four steps to address it.

1: Acknowledge the guilt.

When you realize that you feel guilty about something you're putting off — like not hitting up the gym or socializing with folks around you — I want you to just take a moment and acknowledge the feeling. Recognize your guilt and ask yourself what is making you feel guilty. That leads us to…

2: Use the "five whys" technique.

At the heart of this technique is the question "why?" The idea is that most problems can be solved by asking "why" five times — sometimes even less — and getting to the root issue.

Say you feel guilty because you've not been saying "Hi" to your colleagues in school. You can utilize the technique like this:

Why do I feel guilty?

Because I don't say Hi to them and it seems unfair.

Why haven't I said Hi to them?

Because I don't even know how to approach them or where to start.

Why is that?

Because I find it hard talking to random people.

Why do you find it hard talking to random people?

Because it seems difficult and I have poor social skills.

See what happened? In less than five whys, we figured out why we are having this HUGE issue. With this, we can tackle and solve this issue easily.

3: Write it all down.

Take everything from steps one and two and write it all down — your guilt, each of the whys you asked, and how you can solve everything. This will help you get a clear understanding of how your mind works when it comes to guilt and problem-solving.

It will also give you a good place to go back to when you decide to finally solve the problem — which brings us to….

4: Take action, and take it tomorrow.

That's right. Once you write everything down, I want you

to step back and give it some space.

Do you want to know how to stop procrastinating? It's not by trying to do everything at once.

Because we're humans — and as humans, we are naturally cognitive misers and have limited willpower.

Just doing the five whys and investigating your guilt takes a lot — so just pick it up later when you're fresh and ready to take action. I suggest setting aside some time in a day or two so you don't keep pushing it off.

The next time you find yourself saying something like "I'll get to it later," stop and evaluate why.

Maybe it's not a priority for you right now. Maybe you just don't want to do it. Both of these thoughts are perfectly fine. You'll save everyone a lot of time and effort by recognizing and acting on what's really going on.

Step 3: Change how you describe yourself

It's amazing how often we shoot ourselves in the foot before we can even get started.

This happens when we say things like, "I can't do that because I'm an XYZ-type of person."

Here's a good example: A while back, a friend of mine was talking to me about a girl in his office, and he told me, "I can't talk to her because I'm just an introvert."

I actually got sharp with him. My friend didn't realize that the way he described himself became a self-fulfilling prophecy.

And I was guilty of it too! Back when I looked like this, I used to tell people, "I can't come to the party because I do not like much crowd."

And guess what? That became my reality for YEARS.

ACTION STEP: Reframe the way you talk about yourself.

Quit hiding behind BS-descriptions of yourself as reasons for why you don't do things.

That includes things like:

"I can't make friends because I'm an introvert."

"I'm always going to be out of shape because I'm lazy."

"I can't go into a relationship because I don't hang out much."

Instead, focus on building systems that can help you accomplish your goals — which brings us to…

Step 4: Build systems to accomplish goals

I always get questions along the lines of "How do I find motivation?"

A few insights from these questions:

Motivation is undependable. Waiting for motivation to fall from the sky so you can accomplish your goals is a good way to never get anything done. Why? Because THAT WON'T HAPPEN. You can't wait for your "muse" or "inspiration" to strike.

You need to build the right systems instead. If you asked either of the above people, "What are your steps to accomplish those goals?" they would have no idea how to answer you. That's because it's hard. It's not as appealing as waiting for motivation to strike. However, it's a better approach.

So instead of waiting to be "motivated," take your goal and ask yourself, "What does it take to accomplish my goal?"

And I'm not talking about high-level things like "determination" or "teamwork" or whatever else you find on motivational posters. I'm talking about concrete steps to get there. That will help you develop a solid system for accomplishing your goals.

ACTION STEP: Break down your goal into smaller steps.

Let's take a look at a bad goal and compare it with a good one.

BAD GOAL: "I want to make more friends."

This goal is TERRIBLE. How many people have told themselves this and gotten nowhere? This is because it's vague. There's no concrete action to it. There's not even a way to know when you've accomplished the goal.

Now let's take a look at a better way to approach it.

GOOD GOAL: "I want to make at least four friends a month and hangout 4-5 times with them in a month."

LOVE IT. Notice how I'm focused on the process first by starting off with how many friends I'd want to make in a month. Also, it's only 4-5 times of hangout. That isn't too much time to spend with people that matter.

Do this with your own goals. Maybe you want to be more sociable in school or at your office? Start by talking to one person. Maybe you want a scholarship for school? Start by simply checking out a scholarship book at a library. These small steps will lead to BIG results.

And when you're making these systems, I suggest putting it all on a Google Calendar.

I do this with ALL of my goals.

This is a random to-do that I would normally put in the back of my head, and it would never get done. Instead, I added it to my calendar so it always gets done.

If it's not on my calendar, IT DOESN'T EXIST.

Step 5: Reward yourself for your work

Did you know that talking to random people can help you

improve your social skills?

Seriously, it CAN.

Also, rewarding yourself after a job well done can help create powerful shifts in your mindset.

Something like getting a drink, and a cold bath after hanging out with your colleagues at the end of the day, for example, is a simple way to ignite the reward centers in your brain and cement the good feelings that are required for a habit to take root.

Note: Rewards plays an important role in helping habits stick.

ACTION STEP: Ask yourself, "What habit do I want to start?" and "What will I do to reward myself for taking action?"

Here are a few suggestions to get you started:

Every 25 minutes of deep work you do, give yourself a five-minute break to do whatever you want.

After you hit a savings goal for the month, buy yourself something you want, like a pair of shoes or a video game.

After you hang out with your friends, take in a few episodes of that Netflix show you've been meaning to check out.

The reward can be anything you want — as long as you

genuinely enjoy it.

The truth of procrastinating

If you want to truly stop procrastinating, you have to come to terms with two truths of productivity:

Truth no.1: We all have the same amount of time in the day, so STOP BLAMING TIME (or your lack thereof). It doesn't matter if you're Bill Gates, a busy student or a busy parent. You just need to learn how to manage your time better.

Truth no.2: You don't have to be an emotionless robot in order to stop procrastinating. Focus and time management are about mindsets and simple, yet powerful shifts in how you approach your to-dos.

By adopting the right mindsets, you can create habits that stick instead of struggling to get the simplest of things done.

How To Dominate People

To dominate means to be in control or have the power to defeat.

The ability to dominate people around you is extremely useful in many spheres of life. Whether it's trying to get a resistant woman into bed or getting a potential customer to see you as someone who is more sociable, the art of out-braining the other person is something you'll need.

There are several ways to do this, and the more you use, the better chance you'll have. It's a synergistic effect that builds up until eventually the other person realizes you are the dominant one, stops trying to win, and just gives you what you want.

Here are some of the ways to do it:

1. Have More Conversational Options

There is a saying that goes, "whoever is most flexible controls the communication." In layman's terms, flexibility means the range of your response choices. If you can ask a reframing question, deliberately misinterpret what they said, and logically assert that their statement is wrong, you have far more options than a person who can only respond with "I agree" or "I disagree." You have the bigger arsenal, you have more choice of how to respond, and hence, you are the dominant one.

A related idea is to simply know more about whatever you're talking about than the other person. Whoever has more information wins, because he can pick and choose what to share, in what order, and only give out little bits at a time until he finds the other person's barrier...then brings out the big guns and blasts right through it. You could call this experience, or you could call it knowledge.

2. Persistence

Some people would only buy your product or pay for your service if you are sociable. Some people will not buy no matter what you do or say, and nothing will change that. The skill comes into play with people who want to buy but rationalize all kinds of reasons why they cannot do what you want them to do.

At this point, you have two options. You can say "ok" and back down (i.e., proving that you are the submissive one) or you can persist (demonstrating a belief in the value of your product). You persist by refusing to take "no" for an answer, utilizing a barrage of techniques meant to bring the other person to your point of view without being pushy, rather friendly. The more tools you have, the more you can calibrate the other person's needs to figure out which tools are most appropriate for the job, and this is where Point 1 comes into play.

3. Have Something For Everything

When you've been doing something long enough, whether it's pickup or sales or anything which involves persuasion, there will come a point at which you've heard pretty much everything. Not only have you heard it before, but you've also heard it so many times that you automatically know the best response, since you've had the time and opportunity to practice responses for that exact same scenario, over and over again.

You may still be surprised from time to time, but usually, you know exactly what joke to make, exactly what question to ask, or exactly which idea to probe in order to move the conversation in the direction you want. This is a byproduct of experience, so you need to have hundreds or thousands of similar conversations to get to this place. When you get there, you will casually blow past objections and barriers because you've done it a thousand times before.

4. Listen Carefully

When you listen carefully, you realize that a person will tell you pretty much all you need to know about them to persuade them successfully. If you're selling something and the person tells you they wish they could buy it, but they're putting their kids through school; perfect. Now you know what's important to them: their kids. So you alter your conversation to demonstrate how buying your product helps their kids as well.

People will also tell you, through body language and

"charged" emotion, which topics to avoid in order to successfully persuade them. If you mention kink to a girl and she mentions that she was beaten as a child, it's probably not a good idea to ask whether she prefers being choked or spanked. Yes, I know there are exceptions when broken women enjoy replaying their childhood drama, but I'm talking about most of the time here.

By listening carefully, you learn which paths to persist down and which to avoid altogether.

5. Pay Attention

Similar to Point 4, but more nonverbal. You can tell by subtle changes in vocal tone and body language whether what you're doing is working or not. Persisting at something that is obviously boring the other person just makes you seem uncalibrated, while if you have the ability to notice a sudden "perk" of interest, you know to begin persisting down that path insist.

Most people have no idea what signals they're giving off or how completely obvious their preferences are to anyone who's made the effort to notice and study human behavior. Do it enough and you will shock yourself with how powerful your auto-pilot can be sometimes. There will be situations when, for example, you sell something to a person at an inflated price in 1/10th the time it usually takes you to sell it at the normal price. Such times are proof of your hard work, social skill, and experience, and you may not even consciously be able to dissect what you did.

You just did it. You were in that wonderful "flow" state.

These are some ideas you can use to learn how to dominate other people in a more sociable manner. It is far safer for everyone than exerting your will physically, which can lead to fights and injuries. Far easier to disarm people verbally and with body language, paying close attention to figure out where their triggers are as a guide to where to go.

As I mentioned earlier, the more of these you utilize, the more dominant you will be, and the more expertly you will perform whenever a challenge arises.

Dominant Personality Don't Always Show Aggression

People with strong personalities learn how to socialize in two different ways. In this section, I will show you how dominant people function in social situations.

For example, in many species of animals, the leader of the pack is typically really good at social learning, but this is completely the opposite of what we tend to believe with people. For instance, dominant birds follow other birds that make smart decisions.

It's not a surprise when someone with a strong personality gets what they want out of a social situation, but they do it very strategically. They approach it in a way an animal naturally would. Socially dominant people will either make allies and try to sway others onto their side with solid arguments, while aggressively dominant people will use a more dictatorial type of strategy. If you don't agree with the aggressive personality type, it's "my way or the highway".

It's easy to forget that humans are animals, which is why it makes sense researchers can find similar social strategies in the animal kingdom. After they surveyed people to find out their preferences regarding how to act during social situations, they realized there was a pattern. Those who scored high on questions like "I generally put people in contact with each other" were seen as socially dominant. While people who scored high on questions such as "I like it when other persons serve me" represented an aggressive dominance in social settings.

Although aggressively dominant individuals prefer to rely on their personal experience, well-liked socially dominant individuals are biased toward using information that comes from other people. This shows the positive side of social dominance.

Accurately assessing people's personality types in social settings could be as beneficial as knowing what kind of learner they are. Humans can have so many strengths and weaknesses, and by understanding the full package of a person, students can grow into capable adults more efficiently. People with dominant personalities don't have to be stereotypically uncompromising and bossy. They take control of a situation, are very task oriented, and focused on achieving goals. Just as there must be a leader in a pride of lions, there must be a project manager who naturally, constructively dominates their coworkers.

The more subtle perspective you offer could have important implications for decision-making in both the boardroom and the classroom. For example, if you are trying to help a leader to learn something new it may be important to consider whether they are socially or aggressively dominant and whether they will best learn via a social or individual route.

Building Confidence

Confidence is not something that can be learned like a set of rules; confidence is a state of mind. Positive thinking, practice, training, knowledge and talking to other people are all useful ways to help improve or boost your confidence levels.

Confidence comes from feelings of well-being, acceptance of your body and mind, and belief in your own ability, skills, and experience. Confidence is an attribute that most people would like to possess.

What is Self-Confidence?

Although self-confidence can mean different things to different people, in reality it simply means having faith in yourself.

Confidence is, in part, a result of how we have been brought up and how we've been taught. We learn from others how to think about ourselves and how to behave - these lessons affect what we believe about ourselves and other people. Confidence is also a result of our experiences and how we've learned to react to different situations.

Self-confidence is not a static measure. Our confidence to perform roles and tasks and deal with situations can increase and decrease, and some days we may feel more confident than others.

Low-confidence – This can be a result of many factors including fear of the unknown, criticism, being unhappy with personal appearance (self-esteem), feeling unprepared, poor time-management, lack of knowledge and previous failures. Often when we lack confidence in ourselves, it is because of what we believe others will think of us. Perhaps others will laugh at us or complain or make fun if we make a mistake. Thinking like this can prevent us from doing things we want or need to do because we believe that the consequences are too painful or embarrassing.

Over-confidence – This can be a problem if it makes you believe that you can do anything, even if you don't have the necessary skills, abilities, and knowledge to do it well. In such situations, over-confidence can lead to failure. Being overly confident also means you are more likely to come across to other people as arrogant or egotistical. People are much more likely to take pleasure in your failure if you are perceived as arrogant.

Confidence and self-esteem are not the same thing, although they are often linked. Confidence is the term we use to describe how we feel about our ability to perform roles, functions, and tasks. Self-esteem is how we feel about ourselves, the way we look, the way we think - whether or not we feel worthy or valued. People with low self-esteem often also suffer from generally low confidence, but people with good self-esteem can also have low confidence. It is also perfectly possible for people with low self-esteem to be very confident in some areas.

Performing a role or completing a task confidently is not about not making mistakes. Mistakes are inevitable, especially when doing something new. Confidence includes knowing what to do when mistakes come to light and therefore is also about problem-solving and decision making.

In this section, I have provided you with practical advice about things that you can do to build your confidence and be more sociable.

Ways to Improve Confidence

There are two sides to improving confidence. Although the ultimate aim is to feel more confident in yourself and your abilities, it is also worth considering how you can appear more confident to other people. The following list has lots of ideas on how to achieve this.

- Planning and Preparation

People often feel less confident about new or potentially difficult situations. Perhaps the most important factor in developing confidence is planning and preparing for the unknown.

Here are two examples:

Example I: If you are applying for a new job, it would be a good idea to prepare for the interview. Plan what you would want to say and think about some of the questions that you may be asked. Practice your answers with friends or colleagues and gain their feedback.

Example II: If you are planning to attend a party with your colleagues, and you'd want it to go well, it would be a very nice idea if you prepare for the party. Make plans on what you'd like to say to people at the party, how your movement is going to be at the party. You do not want to go there and start cracking lame jokes and expect people to see you as someone who's sociable.

There are many other examples of planning. Perhaps you should visit the hairdresser before you go. How are you going to drive to the party and how long will it take to get there? What should you wear? Take control of unknown situations the best you can break down tasks into smaller sub-tasks and plan as many as you can.

In some situations, it may be necessary to also have contingency plans - backup plans if your main plan fails. If you had planned to attend the party with your car but in the evening the car wouldn't start, how would you get there? Being able to react calmly to the unexpected is a sign of confidence.

- Learning, Knowledge, and Training

Learning and research can help us to feel more confident about our ability to handle situations, roles, and tasks.

Knowing what to expect and how and why things are done will add to your awareness and usually make you feel more prepared and ultimately more confident.

However, learning and gaining knowledge can sometimes

make us feel less confident about our abilities to perform roles and tasks, and when this happens we need to combine our knowledge with experience. By doing something we have learned a lot about, we put the theory to practice which develops confidence and adds to the learning and comprehension.

First-time lovers to-be may well feel nervous and less than confident about having a relationship. They are likely to buy books or visit websites which can offer advice and dispel some of the mysteries. They are also likely to talk to other people to gain knowledge and understanding.

The same applies to workers. In the workplace, training may be provided for staff to teach them how to manage or work with new systems and procedures. During a period of organizational change, this is particularly important as many people will naturally resist changes. However, if those affected by the changes are given adequate information and training then such resistances can usually be minimized as the staff feel more prepared and therefore more confident with the new system.

- Positive Thought

Positive thought can be a very powerful way of improving confidence.

If you believe that you can achieve something then you are likely to work hard to make sure you do it, however, you don't believe that you can accomplish a task then you are more likely to approach it half-heartedly and therefore be more likely to fail. The trick is convincing yourself that you can do something - with the right help, support, preparedness, and knowledge.

The basic rules of positive thinking are to highlight your strengths and successes and learn from your weaknesses and mistakes. This is a lot easier than it sounds, and we often dwell on things that we are not happy with from our past - making them into bigger issues than they need to be. These negative thoughts can be very damaging to confidence and your ability to achieve goals.

- Try to recondition the way you think about your life

Know your strengths and weaknesses. Write a list of things that you are good at and things that you know need improvement. Discuss your list with friends and family as, inevitably, they will be able to add to the list. Celebrate and develop your strengths and find ways to improve or manage your weaknesses.

We all make mistakes. Don't think of your mistakes as negatives but rather as learning opportunities.

Accept compliments and compliment yourself. When you receive a compliment from somebody else, thank them and ask for more details; what exactly did they like? Recognize your own achievements and celebrate them by rewarding yourself and telling friends and family about them.

Use criticism as a learning experience. Everybody sees the world differently, from their own perspective, and what works for one person may not work for another. Criticism is just the opinion of somebody else. Be assertive when receiving criticism, don't reply in a defensive way or let criticism lower your self-esteem. Listen to the criticism and make sure that you understand what is being said, so you can use criticism as a way to learn and improve.

Try to stay generally cheerful and have a positive outlook on life. Only complain or criticize when necessary and, when you do, do so in a constructive way. Offer others compliments and congratulate them on their successes.

- Talking to Others and Following Their Lead

Ideally, this will be someone that you see regularly, a work colleague, a family member or a friend - somebody with a lot of self-confidence who you'd like to mirror. Observe them and notice how they behave when they are being confident. How do they move, how do they speak, what do they say and when? How do they behave when faced with a problem or a mistake? How do they interact with other people and how do others react to them?

If possible, talk to them to learn more about how they think and what makes them tick.

Speaking to and being around people who are confident will usually help you to feel more confident. Learn from others who are successful in fulfilling the tasks and goals that you wish to achieve - let their confidence rub off on you.

Also, as you become more confident, remember to offer help and advice, become a role model for somebody less confident.

- Experience

As we successfully complete tasks and goals, our confidence that we can complete the same and similar tasks again increase.

A simple example of this is driving a car. Most people who have been driving for some time do so almost automatically - they don't have to think about which peddle to push or how to handle a junction in the road, they just do it. This contrasts to a learner driver who will probably feel nervous and have to concentrate hard. The learner lacks experience and therefore confidence in their ability to drive.

Gaining experience and taking the first step can, however, be very difficult. Often the thought of starting something new is worse than actually doing it. This is where preparation, learning and thinking positively can help.

Break roles and tasks down into small achievable goals. Make each one of your goals fit SMART criteria. That is to make goals Specific, Measurable, Attainable, Realistic and Timed.

Whatever you do, aim to become as good as you can. The better you are at doing something the more confident you become.

- Be Assertive

Being assertive means standing up for what you believe in and sticking to your principles.

Being assertive also means that you can change your mind if you believe it is the right thing to do, not because you are under pressure from somebody else.

Assertiveness, confidence and self-esteem are all very closely linked - usually people become naturally more assertive as they develop their confidence.

- Keep Calm

There is usually a correlation between confidence and calmness.

If you feel confident about a task then you will likely feel calm about doing it. When you feel less confident, you are more likely to be stressed or nervous.

Trying to remain calm, even when you're under stress and pressure, will tend to make you feel more confident.

To do this, it is useful to learn how to relax. Learn at least one relaxation technique that works for you and that you can use if you're feeling stressed. This may be as simple as taking some deliberate deep breaths both in and out.

- Avoid Arrogance

Arrogance is detrimental to interpersonal relationships.

As your confidence grows and you become successful, avoid feeling or acting superior to others. Remember - nobody is perfect and there is always more that you can learn. Celebrate your strengths and successes, and recognise your weaknesses and failures. Give others credit for their work - use compliments and praise sincerely. Be courteous and polite, show an interest in what others are doing, ask questions and get involved.

Also, admit to your mistakes and be prepared to laugh at yourself.

Practicing Your Confidence Skills

Confidence can diminish over time if you don't practise your skills or if you hit setbacks. As you become more confident, you should continue to practise your skills to maintain and boost your confidence further.

Set yourself confidence targets that require you to step out of your comfort zone and do things that make you feel a degree of nervousness or apprehension.

Potential confidence targets may include:

- Starting a task or project that you've been putting off for a long time. Often we put off starting important tasks because they seem overwhelming, difficult or awkward to complete. Simply making a start on such a task can boost confidence and make you more inclined to complete it.

- Making a complaint in a restaurant if there is a problem with your order. If you would not usually complain about a problem when doing so is a good way to improve your confidence and assertiveness skills.

- Standing up to ask a question at a public meeting or in a group. By doing this, you are making yourself the centre of attention for a few minutes.

- Volunteering to give a presentation or make a speech. For many people speaking to a group of people is a particularly scary prospect. The best way to overcome this fear and gain confidence is with experience.

- Introducing yourself to somebody new. This could be a place where people have something in common - like at a party or a conference, making it potentially easier to have a conversation. Or you could talk to a complete stranger in a lift/elevator.

- Wearing something that will draw attention - such as a garish colour. Personal appearance is an important factor in self-esteem and people with lower self-esteem tend to try not to be noticed. Make a statement and stand out in a crowd!

- Joining a group or class in your community. You will potentially benefit from lots of different ways by meeting new local people and learning new things while improving your confidence.

- Taking an unfamiliar journey on public transport. Travelling to a new place using an unfamiliar route and with random people will make most people feel at least slightly uncomfortable. But it is a great way to improve confidence.

Now ask yourself; how do I feel about each of the ideas on the list above? Perhaps some gave you minor feelings of butterflies whereas others filled you with dread. Although the list uses common examples of potentially confidence-boosting tasks, some may not be right for you. Think of some confidence targets that are right for you - then start with easier ones and build up.

Building Confidence Plays a Big Role In Improving your Social skills

Social skills and confidence in social settings don't come naturally to everyone, and that's completely okay! We can't all be the life of the party. One of the best confidence tips is to put yourself out there to meet new people and have even just a simple conversation with them as this can develop your ability to ask questions and make a connection. This boost your social skills drastically.

The more you get used to talking to new people, the easier it will become and the more self-confidence you build. You might actually find that you start to feel enjoyment rather than fear in larger and more diverse situations.

Take a Risk Today

If you're really committed to improving your confidence and social skills, why not take a risk! This will mean something different to everyone, as everyone is at a different stage in developing their skills.

For someone, a risk might be a small step such as saying good morning to the person they stand next to at the bus stop every morning. For someone else, a risk could mean inviting a few people out for a coffee to work on interacting with more than one person at once and finding the confidence to speak amongst a group.

Take Action Today!

Make Friends without Giving Up Who You Are

Making new friends without giving up who you are is really hard to do when you don't know how. Who wants to do something just to wind up struggling and failing?

Also, trying to make new friends when you don't know the reasons why you've been struggling to do it is a lot harder.

That is why I have put together this list of 11 reasons you've had some trouble in this part of your life and what to do about it. Once you see where you've been stuck within any of these common holding patterns below, you can more easily change your approach so you can start building a fulfilling social life today. And yes, you do not have to change/give up who you really are before you can make friends.

Here are 11 Reasons You Have Trouble Making New Friends (And What to do About It)

1. You think making friends should "just happen."

Once we graduate from school, there's not a lot of structures in place to help us along in making new friends. We have to be grown-ups and make those opportunities and structures for ourselves.

This is what I suggest.

I suggest that you come up with a strategy that works for you on finding and making new friends, including showing up at places where you figure people with your interests are already hanging out (When you hang out with people with your interest, you do not have to give up who you are). When you do that, you're not leaving things up to chance, but taking steps to go after what you want. Aside from making more friends, just the practice of taking strategic action feels good in and of itself.

2. You haven't realized yet that making friends is like dating.

The process of making new friends is a lot like dating – you meet someone you like, and you schedule a time to see them again.

For whatever reason, scheduling new-friend-dates happens more rarely than it could. It's normal to feel a little shy when initiating getting together again, but the important thing to remember is that when you feel a spark and genuinely enjoy each other, make a date!

3. You're afraid that initiating conversations will come across as creepy.

What you do for a living shouldn't stop you from making friends or honouring invitations. The truth is, if there's genuine mutual interest and it's a gentle invite, it's not creepy! In fact, my friend and I were talking about this some time ago in the context of dating, and she said of men who have this fear, "If you think you're creepy, that means you're not! Because the truly creepy ones have no idea they're being creepy."

This is pretty funny, and there's definitely some truth in there. Better than worrying about whether or not you're being creepy, focus on noticing whether there's genuine mutual interest there and whether the other person is enjoying you. If he/she is, then they'd probably like to see you again too, so it's not creepy to help them have more of what they want. This goes for dating and friend contexts.

4. You forget your friends have other friends like them.

If you're at a loss for where to find new friends, start with the people you love and respect the most. Organize a small get-together, or if your friend loves to do that kind of thing, offer to co-host. Then, even if you each just invite a couple more people, you're making a great opportunity for new friendships all around.

Bonus points that you're now a connector in your friend's eyes (and in reality), so you're an even more attractive person to get to know. Everyone loves a connector, and it's really not hard to do. It all starts with a small get-together or two, bringing folks together.

5. You pressure yourself to like everyone.

If you're a nice person, you like everyone, right? Certainly, you don't NOT like people. This is what I believed most of my life, anyway.

When I realized I can respect everyone and show kindness without doing backflips over getting to spend time with them, I became much happier and more relaxed. It's okay not to like everyone. You can't possibly, so don't try to force it. If you find you like someone, capitalize on that by setting up "dates" and getting to know them better. Soon, you'll have a budding friendship.

Meanwhile, don't stress when you're not into someone. Still, be kind and respectful, but you're under no obligation to spend time and energy getting to know them if you don't want to. It wouldn't be fair to them anyway. After all, do YOU want anyone befriending you just because they think they should? Yuck, didn't think so.

7. You don't want the chaos and messiness that intimacy can bring.

Don't think that just because you make friends with someone that it's going to be dramatic. It's only dramatic if either (or especially both) of the parties involved are dramatic as well. And you don't have to try being dramatic because your potential friend is dramatic. You can make sure your relationships are full of ease and collaborative by first being an awesome person yourself, and secondly, choosing your friends well.

Be the friend who naturally attracts the kind of friend you want. The same goes for dating, by the way. Be the man/woman who naturally attracts the kind of dates or partner you truly want. YOU DON'T HAVE TO GIVE UP WHO YOU REALLY ARE TO MAKE FRIENDS. NO!

8. You feel shameful about your lack of friends

When we see ourselves as "not social enough" or inherently undesirable, we don't feel (or look) so hot. Just because you don't have as many dear friends as you'd like now, doesn't mean there's anything wrong with you. It simply means you've not identified exactly what you want in a friend and then gone about becoming a natural, intuitive match for that kind of person, and second, not sought out those folks and invited them on friend-dates.

9. You didn't realize that making friends is 95% SKILL and 5% talent.

Does a little talent help? Good looks? Sure. Do you NEED the 5%? No, you don't. Making yourself a more attractive potential friend is a skill. You can make yourself attractive to the kinds of people you're drawn to by taking great care in your presentation, emotional health and happiness, ambition, and everything else.

Skills are learn-able and build-able, and most of life can be dramatically enhanced with skills alone, regardless of any talent that may or may not be there to offer its tiny 5%. We don't often think of talent as so tiny, but it is compared to the monumental force of skill-building. It's just that most of us don't know how to skill-build very well, so we end up noticing and crediting things to talent much more than is warranted.

10. You're a private person and don't want 55 best friends.

Perfect! You don't have to go nuts and spend every waking moment with folks just because you set up one friend-date. Remember that making friends is an inherently gradual process. You decide what kind of social life you want. It's a creative process that is completely up to you, and with time and attention, you can make as many or as few friends as you want. It all boils down to what we want.

11. You've forgotten what you have to offer.

I bet you $250 that you're awesome at something.

Maybe it's something purely social like making people laugh. Maybe it's intellectual or something more strategic, like with your career success. Maybe it's a warmth and cosiness, like baking or homemaking skills.

Whatever you're awesome at can be a GREAT quality to bring to the table in a friendship.

Laughter? That one's obvious. You put people in their happy-endorphin-place.

What about intelligence and success? You can provide reason and objectivity to problems your friends are trying to solve.

Warmth and cosiness? When your friends come to your house, they feel happy, loved, and nourished.

Think about the skills and/or natural disposition you have and how you can start sharing it with new friends.

Then, get cracking at skill-building to fill any missing pieces in your friendship-making process and enjoy what happens.

What You Should Know About Friendship

Friendship is more complex as an adult, especially in your 20's and 30's.

This is the time when people start to make major life decisions like getting married, buying a house or moving across the country to pursue their dreams.

It also happens to be the most important decade for professional success. But a demanding job may limit the time for socializing. Frequent get-togethers may become a thing of the past as you focus on climbing the corporate ladder or leave it behind altogether to blaze an entrepreneurial path.

All of these factors make maintaining relationships– particularly friendships–challenging. Not only is it harder to make new friends when you're crazy busy, but differences in priorities and values may also cause to old bonds to fall apart.

Here's one thing you should know – No matter where your career takes you, relationships are essential to your health and happiness. As you chase your career dreams, you'll inevitably grow personally and professionally. Your friendships will transform as a result.

Keep in mind these four truths to nurture positive connections and reach your professional goals in the process.

- You Get Out What You Put In

If someone's friendship means a great deal to you, it's up to both of you to invest time and resources into keeping the flame alive. That might mean getting a regular Skype date on the calendar with your college roommate or being the one to follow up (yet again) to an email.

Avoid keeping score, but if you're the only one demonstrating effort or you sense the relationships is turning toxic, you may need to re-evaluate the connection and consider moving on.

- Work-Life Balance is an Ongoing Process

While hanging out after school suited friendship-building as a kid, ample free time is in short order as an adult. That means you have to get creative when trying to adapt your social life around your obligations and responsibilities.

Finding the right work-life balance is a challenge every

ambitious person faces, but it's entirely possible to make time for friends even with a chaotic schedule. You can actually put your business skills to work outside of the office to negotiate healthy boundaries, communicate your needs and win the support of those closest to you as you tackle big goals.

- Making Friends as an Adult Takes Time

Opportunities to meet people are everywhere–from the office to industry events, conferences or happy hours. Although you may be interacting with more people, keep in mind that forming deep connections takes time and requires repeated exposure.

Sure, it can be a lengthier process to get to know new colleagues and build rapport, but be patient. If you enjoy someone's company and sense that they return the sentiment, true friendship will come with time as long as you're intentional about growing it.

- It's Okay to Let Go

In today's world, the length of time you've been friends with someone does not correlate with the strength of your friendship with that person. What's important is how the relationship makes you feel right now–not when you were two or twelve years old.

Nevertheless, it can hurt when lifelong friends don't support your career decisions or understand what you do for a living. You may struggle with FOMO (Fear of Missing Out) or feel like you're falling behind while everyone is off accomplishing great things. Emotions like anger, jealousy and resentment can turn toxic and sap your motivation.

How do you know when you're in this situation?

Here's what I advice; do an emotional gut check next time you're with the friend in question or see an update from them on social media. Are you irritated, frustrated, confused, hurt or distant? These red flags can signal it's a good idea to draw the relationship to a close.

Letting a broken relationship fade away if it's not functional or uplifting anymore is not only okay–it's essential to your long-term health and happiness.

Conclusion

The type of social skills that truly improve your life are those that help you get to know other people on a deeper level and help you build real friendships.

Sometimes it's overwhelming to prepare for the future when you aren't even sure what's around the next bend. But don't stress. You now know the ways to prepare for whatever lies ahead even when you don't know what that might be.

Certain life skills—skills you can develop now—will help in almost any situation. They also tend to improve most areas of your life in sometimes obvious, sometimes subtle ways. Bit by bit, you can become more prepared for whatever life throws at you.

These social skills set we've talked about has little to do with popularity.

These skills play a big role in the school, Business, Church callings, dating, meeting your spouse, career, and pretty much everything else you do in life where you might encounter another living person.

For how to improve your social skills, you first have to make this a goal. You have to set your mind to it. This means that you need to learn how to do it, set aside time to practice your skills and make it a point to follow through.

Reading this book won't do it for you automatically. It only gives you the tools that you need to start improving your social skills. Actually using the tools is up to you.

If you work out, you know that when it comes to lifting, if you're not pushing yourself, you're not making changes in your body. The same is true of social skills. If you're not pushing yourself outside of your comfort zone, you're not acquiring the social skills that you want to, the skills that are going to make you highly effective in just about any situation. Remember that getting rid of some of the discomforts that you might have about socializing is part of what you're trying to do by working on your social skills.

There is a significant correlation between your social skills and your success in any area of life. With good social skills, it's easier to make friends, build strong relationships and get ahead in your career.

As someone who lacks social skills, it's essential to follow the steps I have put down in this book, which are:

Managing Shyness,

Improving Your Conversations,

Making Friends Without Giving Up Who You Are

Building Genuine Relationships.

How to Dominate People

Body language

Stopping procrastination. Etc.

Following some (if not all) of the instructions in this book, you will be able to build and improve your social skills in no-time.

As your social skills improve, you'll find yourself feeling more confident in social settings and connecting easier with others. These skills will open up a wide range of opportunities in your life. All you have to do is take advantage of them. Take Action Today. Goodluck!

www.ingramcontent.com/pod-product-compliance
Lightning Source LLC
Chambersburg PA
CBHW070915080526
44589CB00013B/1308